Building Basic Skills in Social Studies

Building Basic Skills in Social Studies

CONTEMPORARY
BOOKS
CHICAGO

Library of Congress Cataloging-in-Publication Data
Main entry under title:

Building basic skills in social studies.

1. Social sciences. 2. Basic education.
I. Contemporary Books, inc.
H91.B84 300 81-803
ISBN 0-8092-5972-9 (pbk.) AACR2

Published by Contemporary Books, Inc.
Two Prudential Plaza, Chicago, Illinois 60601-6790
Manufactured in the United States of America
International Standard Book Number: 0-8092-5972-9

ACKNOWLEDGMENTS

The thoughtful efforts of a great many people went into the preparation of Contemporary Books' *Building Basic Skills* series. We gratefully acknowledge their contributions and continued involvement in Adult Education.

Adult Education Division

Lillian J. Fleming, Editorial Director
Barbara Drazin, Editor
Wendy Harris, Marketing Services Coordinator

Production Department

Deborah Eisel, Production Editor

Reading and Readability Editors

Jane L. Evanson
Helen B. Ward
Norma Libman
Deborah Nathan
Jane Friedland
Donna Wynbrandt

Authors and Contributors

Writing: Rob Sax

Social Studies: Robert Schambier
Carol Hagel
Phil Smolik
Jack Lesar
Nora Ishibashi
Helen T. Bryant
Jo Ann Kawell
Deborah Brewster
Mary E. Bromage
Sheldon B. Silver
Patricia Miripol

Project Assistance
Sara Plath

Science: Ronald LeMay
Cynthia Talbert
Jeffrey Miripol
John Gloor
William Collien
Charles Nissim-Sabat

Reading: Timothy A. Foote
Raymond Traynor
Pamela D. Drell (Editor)

Mathematics: Jerry Howett

Graphic Art: Louise Hodges
Cover Design: Jeff Barnes

CONTENTS

TO THE LEARNER

Building Basic Skills in Social Studies from Contemporary Books is planned with you the learner in mind. Your work in this book will start to build your social studies knowledge while it gives you practice building your reading skills.

HOW TO GET THE MOST FROM THIS BOOK

TAKE THE PRE-TEST

A good way to start your work in *Building Basic Skills in Social Studies* is to take the **Pre-Test.** The 35 questions will give you a good idea of your strengths before you start to work. The reading passages and questions on the Pre-Test will also give you a feel for what's coming in the book.

The Pre-Test is made up of social studies reading passages followed by reading skill questions. There are also questions that follow cartoons, graphs or charts. Finally, we have also put in some social studies questions that stand alone. These will tell what you already know about some social studies topics. In working all the questions, remember that there is no time limit. You may take as much time as you need. Remember that the Pre-Test is meant to be a way to show where your skills are *before* you begin building them. Afterwards, the Post-Test will show how much your work has paid off.

CHECK YOUR PRE-TEST ANSWERS

RECORD YOUR SCORE

You will be able to check your work using the **Answers and Explanations** that follow the Pre-Test. The reading and social studies skills needed for each question are shown here too. Finally, remember to record your score on the **Pre-Test Skill Record** (page 20).

Five units of social studies make up this skill-building book. They are:

WORK THROUGH THE FIVE SOCIAL STUDIES UNITS

Economics—the study of how goods and services are produced, distributed and used

Geography—the study of the earth's land, water and air including how plants and animals live on the earth

Political Science—the study of how governments form and work

History—everything that people have ever done and the story or record of these events

Behavioral Science—the study of how and why people act, think and feel as they do—alone and in social groups

Each unit is made up of reading passages that are written about different topics. Working through the passages will build both your reading skills and your knowledge.

STUDY THE KEY WORDS

A list of **Key Words** comes before each reading passage. These words give you an idea of what the passage is about. They are used in the passage along with other words that may be new to you.

USE THE GLOSSARY

We have listed many words that may be new (and all of the Key Words) in the helpful Glossary at the end of the book. The **Glossary** gives the meanings of words and is a good tool for reviewing what you learned from the passages.

Five reading skill questions follow each social studies passage. These questions have been written to build your reading skills. They follow this plan:

ANSWER THE READING SKILL QUESTIONS

First Reading Skill Question	Finding the main idea of the passage
Second Reading Skill Question	Recalling a supporting detail
Third Reading Skill Question	Applying facts and ideas
Fourth Reading Skill Question	Making inferences
Fifth Reading Skill Question	Drawing a conclusion from the passage

Each kind of reading skill question asks you to use a different kind of thinking to answer the question. We should tell you more about the skills:

MAIN IDEA

The main idea is what the passage is about. It is made up of a topic and what is then said about the topic. It is the important point that the writer wants the reader to understand. Most of the facts, or details, in the passage relate to the main idea. The main idea of a social studies reading passage is often found near the beginning. The main idea also may be repeated at the end of the passage.

DETAILS

Details, or facts, support the main idea. They add to it and give it more meaning. You have to pay attention to details, even small ones. They do count.

APPLICATION

Application of information is a reading skill very different from finding the main idea or supporting details. It means that you use what you learn from reading the passage. You apply that knowledge to a new situation.

INFERENCE

Making inferences means that you read between the lines of what the writer directly says. You use what the writer *says* to find out what he or she *means*. The words "suggest" and "imply" often mean that you are being asked to make an inference.

CONCLUSION

Drawing a conclusion is like answering the question "so what?" after reading the passage. A conclusion sums up part of the writer's message. It is a brief statement that pulls together the writer's main idea, supporting details and inferences.

CHOOSE THE BEST ANSWER

Each reading skill question is followed by five answer choices. You are asked to choose the one that is the BEST answer to the question. Remember to read all five choices before you choose your answer.

CHECK YOUR ANSWERS

When you are ready to check your answers, use the **Answers and Explanations** at the end of each unit. Each answer is explained so that you will know why it is the BEST answer.

Building these five skills is a first step in mastering social studies reading. *Building Basic Skills in Social Studies* will give you good practice finding the main idea, using supporting details, applying information, making inferences and drawing conclusions.

START A NOTEBOOK OF MAIN IDEAS

It's a good idea to get a notebook and write down every main idea you work with in this book. Explain the idea in your own words. Use some of the details from the passage. You also might want to jot down the Key Words and what they mean. A notebook like this is a good tool for learning anything and may help make the areas of social studies "belong" to you. Ideas from TV, radio, movies, newspapers and magazines may be included. Look at the picture that shows how a page from your notebook might look.

Starting a notebook of main ideas

TAKE THE POST-TEST

After you have worked through all the passages and the questions, take the **Post-Test.** Like the Pre-Test, the Post-Test is made up of 35 questions from all five units. There are questions that follow reading passages and some that follow cartoons, graphs or charts. There are also questions that stand alone to test your knowledge in economics, geography, political science, history or behavioral science.

CHECK YOUR POST-TEST ANSWERS

RECORD YOUR SCORE

You'll be able to check your answers as you did with the Pre-Test. The **Answers and Explanations** list the reading and social studies skills you used. If you had trouble with one kind of reading skill, go back through the book and practice. You'll get better at it. Finally, record your score using the **Post-Test Skill Record** (page 162).

YOUR NEXT STEP

Once you have finished this book, you'll be ready to go on. Your teacher will probably be able to work with you on what to do next. If you're studying for the GED test, you can easily move on to Contemporary's *GED Test 2: The Social Studies Test*. It's like this book but it gives more difficult reading passages and more practice answering questions.

Whatever your next step, we hope you always keep building your skills. Learning is a lifelong experience!

The Editors of Contemporary Books

PRE-TEST

Directions: **The Pre-Test is made up of 35 questions from economics, geography, political science, history and behavioral science. It's a good way to get an idea of how you will work in this book. It will give you an idea of topics in social studies and of social studies reading skills.**

There are three types of questions. Some follow a short reading passage. Read each passage and answer the questions based on what you read. Other questions stand alone. To answer these questions, you have to use your own experience or prior knowledge. The third type of question comes after a cartoon, a graph or a chart. Answer these questions based on what you understand from looking at the cartoon, graph or chart.

There is no time limit. If you don't know an answer, try to figure it out. You can even guess at some answers. Read all five choices. Then put a check mark (✓) next to the BEST answer for each question. When you finish answering the 35 questions, check your answers with the Answers and Explanations section that follows. Circle each correct answer. Then turn to page 20 to fill in the Pre-Test Skill Record.

Some experts think that intelligence comes mostly from what you inherit from your parents. Others think it develops from your experiences in life. This difference has been called the "nature" versus "nurture" question. There is a great debate about just what is caused by heredity and what comes from what we learn growing up.

People who support the "nature" side say that heredity is the main key to intelligence. They feel that no amount of teaching could make an Albert Einstein or a Paul Robeson. One must be born with the ability to learn science or music and other areas as these men did. According to the "nature" side of the debate, the genes control the level a person can reach.

The "nurture" side believes that intelligence is changed by a person's environment, experiences and surroundings. They say that a person with great intelligence must have been exposed to the right things to cause that growth. They see the mind at birth as a blank page. It can be filled in by those experiences which lead to learning. The environment or "nurture" side of the debate states that life experiences, education and training are the key.

Many psychologists take a balanced view. They say that both factors are important. Together, heredity and environment—"nature" and "nurture"—can affect what a person is able to do in life.

1. "Nature" as used in this passage means
   ______(1) wild animals and plants
   ______(2) a person's basic character
   ______(3) learning ability
   ______(4) heredity
   ______(5) environment

2. Which idea from the passage might lead parents to send their children to pre-school?
   ______(1) there is a great debate about the role of heredity and environment
   ______(2) the right experiences can increase intelligence
   ______(3) no amount of teaching could make an Einstein or a Robeson
   ______(4) genes control the level one can reach
   ______(5) psychologists take a balanced view

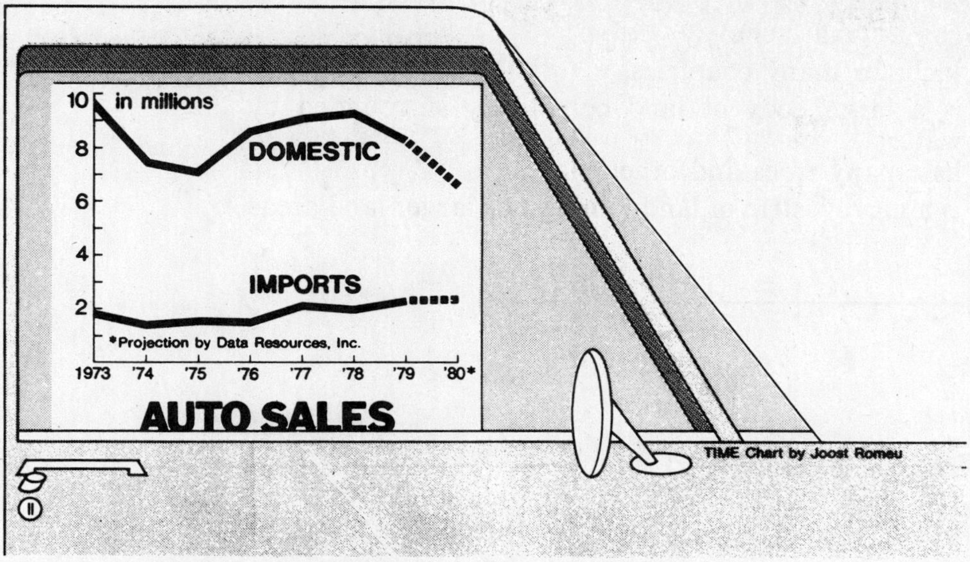

3. If the trend goes on as the chart suggests, we may expect that

______(1) we will see more foreign cars on the highways
______(2) American car dealers will make more money
______(3) fewer cars will be imported in coming years
______(4) more American cars will be made
______(5) the total number of cars sold will increase

____

4. The total dollar value of all goods and services produced in the nation in a given year is called

______(1) the Dow Jones Index
______(2) the Gross National Product
______(3) the Consumer Price Index
______(4) the money balance
______(5) supply and demand

____

5. Central America is an isthmus. This means that it
   ______(1) has a canal zone
   ______(2) includes many countries
   ______(3) is a large body of land completely surrounded by water
   ______(4) has many trees and other plants
   ______(5) is a narrow strip of land joining two larger land areas

---

The main job of the Congress of the United States is to make laws. Congress is made up of the Senate and the House of Representatives. Both chambers or bodies are part of the law-making process. But some jobs have to be done by one chamber alone. This is stated in the Constitution. For example, the House of Representatives must bring up all bills to spend money. It is a job of the Senate to approve or reject these bills. The House of Representatives must also approve or reject bills started in the Senate.

The Senate, the higher chamber, has two senators from each state. They serve six-year terms. Their terms end in different years so that one-third of the Senate runs for re-election every two years.

A candidate for the Senate must be at least 30 years old. The candidate must be a legal resident of the state where he or she is running. This person must have been a U.S. citizen for at least nine years.

Membership in the House, the lower chamber, is based on state population. Each state has at least one representative, and the large states have many. California, for instance, has 38. When a state's representatives work together their state has a strong voice in Congress.

To run for the House, a person must be at least 25 years old, a citizen for at least seven years, and a resident of the state in which elected.

Each member of Congress has two roles. On the one hand the member must meet the needs of his or her own state. But, on the other hand, he or she must work for the good of the whole nation.

6. The passage says that a senator
   ______(1) may not run for re-election
   ______(2) serves a six-year term
   ______(3) is also a representative
   ______(4) must be at least 25 years old
   ______(5) cannot have been born in a foreign country

7. The fact that the House is called the lower chamber implies that
   ______(1) it has fewer members than the Senate
   ______(2) its members make no important laws
   ______(3) its members have less power than senators
   ______(4) the chamber is often located below the upper chamber
   ______(5) its members have shorter terms than senators

8. Judging from the passage, you should vote for a candidate who
   ______(1) is a loyal party member
   ______(2) is older than 25
   ______(3) supports local views only
   ______(4) has money
   ______(5) knows about national concerns

9. According to the passage, which of the following states will have the fewest representatives in the House, or lower chamber?
   ______(1) California
   ______(2) Illinois
   ______(3) Alaska
   ______(4) New York
   ______(5) Michigan

10. Which of the following did NOT have to do with slavery in America?

_____(1) the Boston Tea Party
_____(2) the Missouri Compromise
_____(3) the Dred Scott Decision
_____(4) the Abolition Movement
_____(5) the Civil War

We often hear people using the words personality and character. Many people think they are one and the same. Actually they are quite different. Personality can be thought of as the way one appears to others or "comes across." It reflects how a person feels toward and gets along with other people.

Character, on the other hand, has to do with a person's outlook on life. It is a measure of moral traits or what a person believes is right and wrong. Beliefs and attitudes rest in one's character, no matter what the personality may suggest. A shy person may have a clear sense of right and wrong and thus have strong character. In contrast, a friendly person may be self-assured when meeting new people. The same person may feel unsure about right and wrong.

11. The writer says that character

_____(1) is not as important as personality
_____(2) has mostly to do with feelings
_____(3) cannot be changed
_____(4) is based on moral beliefs
_____(5) is the same as personality

12. A course on "How to Win Friends and Influence People" would be likely to

_____(1) help strengthen one's values
_____(2) help develop one's personality

______(3) help a person know his own beliefs
______(4) help improve one's outlook on life
______(5) help build character

---

13. A government raises the price of its imported steel to equal the price of its domestic steel. This is called a(n)
______(1) sales tax
______(2) competitive tariff
______(3) negative income tax
______(4) embargo
______(5) deferred payment

14. The map shows that the two Korean capitals are
______(1) the same distance from China
______(2) both in the demilitarized zone (D.M.Z.)
______(3) about 1500 miles apart
______(4) less than 200 miles apart
______(5) south of the Yellow Sea

Mexico had a well-developed culture long before Columbus came to the New World. Today, much of Mexico shows a Spanish influence. This is because the early explorers forced their culture on the native Indians living there. But even though the Spanish conquered the Indians, Indian culture survived. Today, Mexico is a blend of Spanish and Indian ways.

The Spanish language is used by most people. It is colored by many Indian words. About 50 Indian languages, including Mayan and Aztec, are still spoken.

The contrasts between the two cultures can still be seen in Mexico. But now in Mexico's busy cities there are also modern skyscrapers, businesses, stores and many cars. It is not odd to see a modern apartment building crowding out a beautiful old Spanish church or early Indian ruins. Somehow, the new buildings cannot quite capture the richness of the old. Progress and technical advances are happening in Mexico. Hopefully, they will not destroy the rich Indian and Spanish heritage of the country.

15. The language most used in Mexico is

______(1) a mix of Indian languages
______(2) English with Spanish words
______(3) a language used before Columbus came to the New World
______(4) Spanish with Indian words added
______(5) Aztec and Mayan

16. From the passage, the reader might think that Mexican culture

______(1) has kept nothing from the days before the Spanish
______(2) has fewer problems than other cultures
______(3) could be spoiled by technical change and modern advances
______(4) is the same as that of Spain
______(5) is controlled by the government

17. Judging by Mexico's history, a well-developed culture

______(1) survives even when other cultures are forced on the nation
______(2) will have old churches and Indian ruins

______(3) will not accept new ideas
______(4) is more quickly changed by other groups
______(5) needs many languages

---

18. A peer group is
______(1) mass actions in a culture
______(2) a religious club or cult
______(3) all the people of a nation
______(4) persons who have political power
______(5) persons alike in age, grade or status

Although it happened half a century ago, stories are still told about Wall Street's crash in 1929. The nation had been through financial scares before, but nothing to match the "Great Depression." The collapse came in late October, 1929. The depression was the major event of the 1930s.

No single cause led to the stock market fall. The day it happened is now called "black Tuesday." Some people tried to blame the president. But Herbert Hoover was not at fault for the tragic event. It involved many economic factors such as production, wages, loans and trade.

The United States was not alone in the hard years that followed the stock market crash. Great Britain, too, went through business problems and failures. By 1931, the depression had become so severe in Europe that world trade had almost stopped.

In the presidential election of 1932, American voters expressed their desire for change. They elected Franklin D. Roosevelt. F.D.R. promised America a "New Deal." Banking and investment reforms were part of the New Deal. The New Deal also included controls over how much factories produced and laws to protect consumers. The Social Security program and minimum wage standards began during the New Deal.

The election of 1932 helped Americans to gain new faith in themselves. Slowly the economy improved. As people began to have more hope for the future they spent more money. Business increased and more people found jobs. Banks once more began making loans and recovery was on the way.

19. This passage is mainly about

_____(1) the Great Depression and America's recovery
_____(2) the start of the Social Security program
_____(3) the many causes of economic problems
_____(4) the need for a strong leader
_____(5) the importance of the "New Deal"

20. The "New Deal" was

_____(1) Roosevelt's plan for dealing with the depression
_____(2) a new trade agreement with Europe
_____(3) a new election system
_____(4) a set of price controls to give a better deal on goods
_____(5) Hoover's set of rules which caused the stock market crash

21. The passage suggests that the U.S. economy

_____(1) has to do with production and wages only
_____(2) is not affected by world events
_____(3) always protected consumers
_____(4) should stay away from world trade
_____(5) is related to political leadership and confidence

A referendum is a question placed on the ballot after legislators have passed it. It then becomes an issue for the people's vote. This is done when the question is one of broad concern, such as that of changing a state constitution. In this case, the citizens of a state get to vote on a change in their basic law. If a referendum is an amendment to a state constitution, a two-thirds majority vote is usually needed for it to pass. This helps to prevent a small group or a private interest from making changes not wanted by the public.

22. A referendum is

_____(1) an issue decided by direct popular vote
_____(2) an amendment to a state constitution
_____(3) the same as an election
_____(4) a two-thirds majority vote
_____(5) needs of a private interest group

23. Which of the following would most likely be a referendum question?

_____(1) Should a political rally be held?
_____(2) Should the federal budget be balanced?
_____(3) Should the number of members of the state senate change?
_____(4) Should the president be impeached?
_____(5) Should Congress adjourn early?

The Consumer Price Index (C.P.I.) measures changes in the cost of living. The percent of a worker's pay that is needed to buy certain goods is figured. This percent is compared with the percent of a person's wages needed to buy the same goods in the past. For example, if you hear that the Consumer Price Index for food has gone up, you know that people are paying a larger share of their earnings for food than they were in the past.

24. If the cost of food, clothing, housing and transportation rises over a 10-year period, but the C.P.I. stays the same, you may conclude that

_____(1) inflation has cut down the value of the dollar
_____(2) the consumer must work longer for each item bought

______(3) prices have changed at about the same rate as wages
______(4) goods cost less now than they did ten years ago
______(5) too many goods are being produced for consumer needs

---

25. "Lame duck" sessions in Congress occur

______(1) before an election
______(2) after an election
______(3) when the president is absent
______(4) when there aren't enough congressmen for a vote
______(5) after a bill is vetoed

Climate is very important in deciding where and how people live. Most of the world's people live where temperatures aren't too hot or too cold, where there is plenty of rain and where soil is good for growing food. But people also live where the climate is very harsh. One approach to geography is to study the climate zones of the world and how climate affects human beings.

One climate zone is the tropical dry lands. In this zone, the weather is hot and dry. This is desert land that has little plant and wildlife. Life in these regions of the world is harsh. Such areas have given rise to a nomadic life-style. Nomads are groups of people that wander from place to place in search of food and water instead of settling in one place. Tropical dry lands are found in Asia, northern Africa, and the southwest part of the United States, Mexico, Peru, Chile and Australia. The Sahara Desert in northern Africa is the largest single area of dry land. It covers about three million square miles.

In contrast to the tropical dry lands, the sunny semi-tropical zone is comfortable. The areas around the Mediterranean Sea and the California coastline are examples. These areas have a pleasant climate where fruit can be grown. People enjoy life in these zones and so the populations are usually large.

The polar zones are the coldest parts of the earth. There are two types of polar climate. The tundra regions have some plant life. The extreme northern parts of North America, Europe and Asia have tundra regions. The polar ice-cap regions, on the other hand, have freezing temperatures year-round and no plant life. Ice-capped Antarctica is a polar land where there is ice and snow all year long.

26. The main idea of this passage is
   ______(1) geography is the study of climate
   ______(2) people like tropical dry lands better than polar areas
   ______(3) climate affects where and how people live
   ______(4) there are more dry than wet climate zones
   ______(5) nomads live where climate is harsh

27. Climate is
   ______(1) how hot or cold a region is
   ______(2) the amount of plant and wildlife in an area
   ______(3) the number of people living in a place
   ______(4) the weather pattern of a region
   ______(5) the rain or lack of rain in a certain zone

28. The tundra region
   ______(1) is part of the polar ice cap
   ______(2) is probably thinly populated
   ______(3) is part of the desert
   ______(4) is one of the semi-tropical zones
   ______(5) is in the southern United States

The Industrial Revolution caused many changes in the United States. The promise of work and of profits brought many farm people into the cities. Urban areas grew, while the number of farms fell. America's life-style moved away from what is called subsistence farming. People began to depend on money and a cash economy. They wanted to earn money and to have enough to buy the goods that the modern technology of the Industrial Revolution could produce. The graph shows the percent of farm and non-farm workers in the United States between 1840 and 1920.

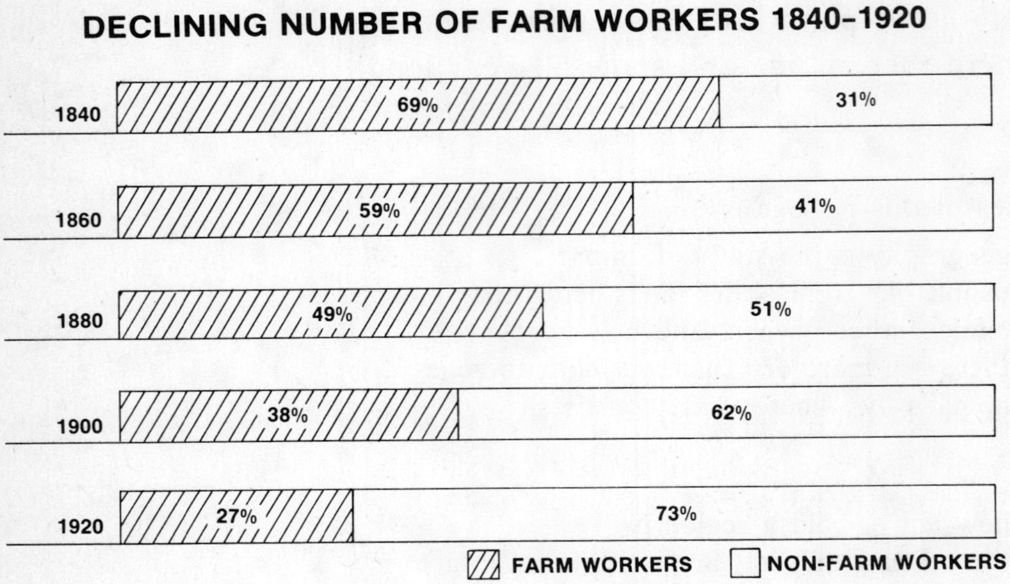

29. From 1840 to 1920, the number of non-farm workers for each twenty years grew about
______(1) 10 percent
______(2) 31 percent
______(3) 69 percent
______(4) 73 percent
______(5) 100 percent

30. The ratio of farm to non-farm workers in 1840 and 1920 was
______(1) twice as many farm workers by 1920
______(2) about the same numbers both years
______(3) about opposite for the two years, with non-farm workers increasing

______(4) 73% more non-farm than farm workers by 1920
______(5) about one-fourth as many farm workers in 1920 as there were in 1840

31. Subsistence farming means
______(1) farming to produce one's own food
______(2) using large farms
______(3) depending on cash to run a farm
______(4) farming based on technology
______(5) avoiding urban regions

The United States Constitution was written in 1787. It sets the basic principles of our government. Amendments, or changes, make it possible for the Constitution to meet needs that come up as society grows. An amendment becomes part of the Constitution when it is passed by Congress and by three-fourths of the states.

The first ten amendments to the Constitution are called the Bill of Rights. These protect people against wrongs which could come from bad government rule. They limit the power of the nation's government to make laws which could destroy states' rights or deny the freedom of individuals. The Bill of Rights assures freedom of speech, the right to privacy, and the right to jury trials, among other rights.

32. According to the passage, one might expect that
______(1) the Constitution may soon be replaced as our basic law
______(2) the Constitution will continue to be our basic law
______(3) the Constitution will not need any more amendments
______(4) the U.S. government will come to depend less on the Constitution
______(5) some states will refuse to obey the Constitution

33. The Bill of Rights is the name for
______(1) all Constitutional amendments
______(2) laws that deal with the court system
______(3) the first ten amendments to the U.S. Constitution
______(4) America's first set of laws
______(5) the Declaration of Independence

A corporation is a group of people licensed to act as one legal body. It can do business in its own name, enter into contracts and earn profits. It may own property and it may sue or be sued as a result of its acts. Since a corporation is collectively owned, however, no one member can be forced to pay its debts. In short, a corporation may do anything that one person may legally do but it protects its members from total financial responsibility.

34. If you were to start a for-profit corporation, one advantage you could expect would be
______(1) your own personal money would be safer
______(2) the corporation would not have to pay taxes
______(3) you would be more likely to make a profit
______(4) the corporation could not go bankrupt
______(5) the corporation would be protected from lawsuits

---

35. During the American Bicentennial in 1976, America celebrated
______(1) the date of the first Constitutional Convention
______(2) the end of World War II
______(3) the first Veteran's Day
______(4) 100 years without war
______(5) its 200th birthday

ANSWERS AND EXPLANATIONS—PRE-TEST

DETAIL 1. **(4)** is correct. The writer tells you that those who support the "nature" side think that heredity is the key.

APPLICATION 2. **(2)** is correct. If the right environment can increase intelligence, then it would make sense to train children early.

CONCLUSION 3. **(1)** is the best answer. The sales trend is downward for American-made cars. Sales of imports or foreign cars are rising. You can conclude that since more foreign cars are being sold in the U.S. more will be seen on our highways.

PRIOR KNOWLEDGE 4. **(2)** is the correct answer. There was nothing to help you find this answer. You must have already known the meanings.

PRIOR KNOWLEDGE 5. **(5)** is the correct answer. You can look on a map and see that this is true.

DETAIL 6. **(2)** is correct. It is stated in the second paragraph.

INFERENCE 7. **(3)** is the best answer. Since the passage does not explain this, you must figure it out. The fact that some states have large numbers of representatives gives you the clue that each may have less power than do members of the smaller Senate.

APPLICATION 8. **(5)** is the best answer. The last sentence points out that a member of Congress must work for the good of the whole nation.

INFERENCE 9. **(3)** is the correct answer. Alaska's population is lower than any of the other states listed. Therefore, it must have fewer representatives.

PRIOR KNOWLEDGE 10. **(1)** is the correct answer. The Boston Tea Party was a protest. The American colonists dumped tea into the harbor because they did not want to keep paying taxes to England. It had no direct connection to slavery in the U.S.

DETAIL 11. **(4)** is the correct answer. This is explained at the beginning of the second paragraph.

APPLICATION 12. **(2)** is the best answer. The passage says that personality relates to how we get along with people. A course like this would deal with that topic.

PRIOR KNOWLEDGE — 13. **(2)** is correct. Tariffs are taxes on imports and this one keeps the price of foreign steel in line with the price of domestic steel. This keeps the two prices competitive.

APPLICATION — 14. **(4)** is correct. You must know that the stars mean capital cities. Then you must use the scale in the lower left corner to judge the distance between the two cities.

DETAIL — 15. **(4)** is correct. This fact is stated in the second paragraph.

INFERENCE — 16. **(3)** is the best answer. The writer ends with a cautious note about technical advance. He says that progress is happening in Mexico, but seems to be worried about what this may do to Mexico's rich culture.

INFERENCE — 17. **(1)** is the best answer. The writer gives details to support the idea that some of the Indian culture still remains.

PRIOR KNOWLEDGE — 18. **(5)** is the correct answer. A peer group is a group of people who have age, grade or status in common.

MAIN IDEA — 19. **(1)** is the best answer. All of the others are details that are part of the main idea.

DETAIL — 20. **(1)** is correct. This is stated in the second paragraph from the end.

INFERENCE — 21. **(5)** is the best answer. The last paragraph shows what happened as people began to feel more hopeful.

INFERENCE — 22. **(1)** is correct. You can figure this out from the information given at the beginning of the passage.

APPLICATION — 23. **(3)** is the best answer. It deals with a basic state law. (1) is not a broad enough issue. All of the others are powers of Congress.

APPLICATION — 24. **(3)** is the correct answer. Since the passage says that the Consumer Price Index tells the percent of a worker's pay needed to buy certain goods, you can figure this out. When the index remains the same, it means that prices and wages are at the same ratio to each other.

PRIOR KNOWLEDGE — 25. **(2)** is the correct answer. The "lame ducks" are those who did not win or are leaving office, but still have to finish out the term.

MAIN IDEA — 26. **(3)** is correct. The first line gives you the idea. Each discussion of zones also talks about climate and population.

INFERENCE 27. **(4)** is correct. (1) and (5) are only parts of the answer. (2) and (3) are effects of climate.

INFERENCE 28. **(2)** is the correct answer. You can figure this out from the information in the passage.

DETAIL 29. **(1)** is the correct answer. You can note that the figures go from 31 to 41, 51, 62, 73.

DETAIL 30. **(3)** is the correct answer. You can see this by looking at the graph for the years 1840 and 1920.

INFERENCE 31. **(1)** is the correct answer. You can figure this out from the fact that farmers were moving to cities and becoming more dependent on a cash economy. Those who raised their own food would not depend so much on having money.

CONCLUSION 32. **(2)** is the best answer. The passage points out that the Constitution can adapt as needs change. It also says that we've followed it since 1787.

DETAIL 33. **(3)** is correct. This is stated in the first line of the second paragraph.

APPLICATION 34. **(1)** is the best answer. The passage tells you that a corporation can act as one, but that no one member would be responsible for its debts. This means you risk less.

PRIOR KNOWLEDGE 35. **(5)** is the correct answer. Two hundred years had passed since America declared its independence from Britain in 1776. Centennial means 100th anniversary and "bi" means two or, in this case, two times 100.

PRE-TEST ANSWER KEY

1. **(4)**	8. **(5)**	15. **(4)**	22. **(1)**	29. **(1)**
2. **(2)**	9. **(3)**	16. **(3)**	23. **(3)**	30. **(3)**
3. **(1)**	10. **(1)**	17. **(1)**	24. **(3)**	31. **(1)**
4. **(2)**	11. **(4)**	18. **(5)**	25. **(2)**	32. **(2)**
5. **(5)**	12. **(2)**	19. **(1)**	26. **(3)**	33. **(3)**
6. **(2)**	13. **(2)**	20. **(1)**	27. **(4)**	34. **(1)**
7. **(3)**	14. **(4)**	21. **(5)**	28. **(2)**	35. **(5)**

PRE-TEST SKILL RECORD

Directions: Fill in the Pre-Test Skill Record after you have taken the Pre-Test and have checked your answers. The Skill Record will show your strengths in social studies reading skills and prior knowledge.

PRE-TEST DATE: ____________________

Pre-Test Skills	Total Questions	Test Questions	Number Correct
• Finding the Main Idea	2	19,26	
• Recalling Details	8	1,6,11,15, 20,29,30,33	
• Applying Information	7	2,8,12,14 23,24,34	
• Making Inferences	9	7,9,16,17,21, 22,27,28,31	
• Drawing Conclusions	2	3,32	
• Using Prior Knowledge	7	4,5,10,13, 18,25,35	
TOTAL	**35**	**TEST SCORE**	

UNIT I: ECONOMICS

Economics is the study of how goods and services are produced, distributed and used.

Directions: **The following passages cover topics in economics. Each one starts with one or more Key Words. The Key Words will give you an idea of what the passage is about. They are also used in the passage along with other words that might be new. You will be able to figure out the meanings of some new words as you read them in the passage. Look up any word that is new in the Glossary at the end of the book, or use a dictionary.**

After each passage, there are five reading skill questions to answer. Make a check (✓) next to the BEST answer for each question. Be sure to read all five choices first.

The Answers and Explanations begin on page 42.

ECONOMICS PASSAGE 1

KEY WORDS

value—(noun) the worth, fair price or cost of something

law of supply and demand—(noun) a basic law of economics that says value is related to how much of something is available (supply) and how many people want it (demand)

Economics is the study of how goods and services are produced and distributed. It is also the study of the value of different goods and services and how those values change. Economists have come up with some basic laws that show how our system and others work.

To live, people need food, clothing, housing and many other products or goods. We all need the services of doctors, teachers, carpenters and lots of other people. These goods and services cost money.

Money, in turn, is earned by making and selling goods and services. A doctor, for example, makes money by charging fees for medical care. General Motors makes money by making and selling cars. An auto worker there makes money by selling his or her services as a worker to the company. These are just a few ways people and companies make money.

A basic law of economics is the law of supply and demand. This law explains the value of goods and services in terms of how much of something is available (supply) and how many people want to buy it (demand). Here's an example: an unexpected cold spell ruined much of the Florida orange crop during the winter of 1980. All around

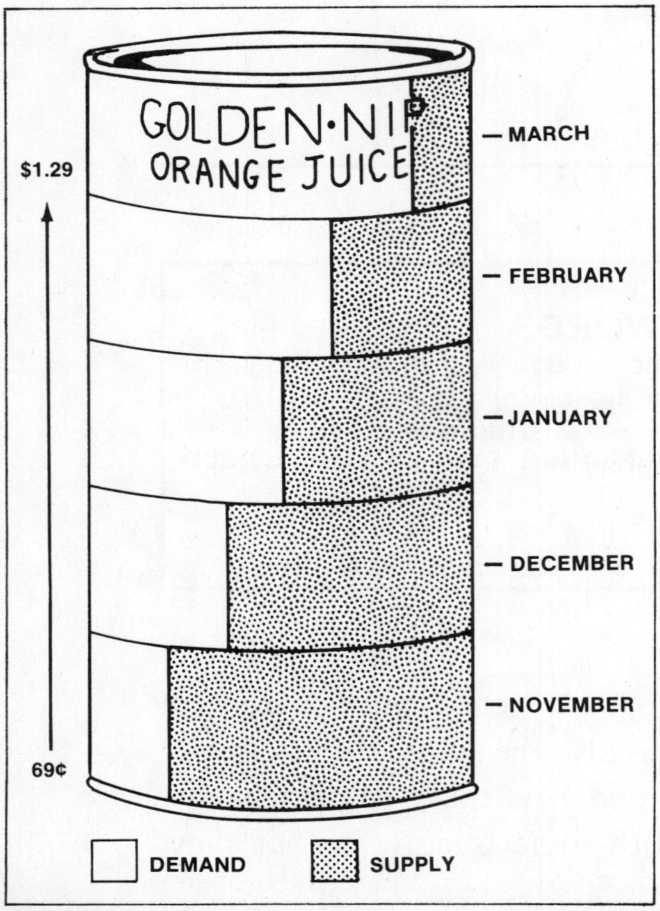

We pay more when supplies are low and demand is high.

the country supplies of fresh and frozen orange juice dwindled. In grocery stores, prices shot up. In some places a 12-ounce can of frozen orange juice went from 69¢ to $1.29. The supply was not enough to match the demand. So prices went up. The price of frozen orange juice will remain high until the damage to the crops is overcome or until orange crops from other states, like California, make up for the Florida losses.

The law of supply and demand says that when supplies are low and demand is high, prices will be higher. When demand goes down and supplies go up, prices are usually lower. Value, cost and prices depend on supply and demand.

Even money follows the law of supply and demand. When a great deal of money is in circulation—being spent—the money's value goes down. People have to pay more for what they buy. This lowering of money's value is called inflation.

If the value of a country's money goes down by 10%, we say the level of inflation is 10%. That means that the money will buy 10% less than it did before inflation struck.

Economists say there must be a balance between supply and demand for people and nations to get the goods and services they want. To achieve that balance, they say, workers must be productive and consumers must be able to buy what they need.

We study economics to learn about societies—why some are rich and others are poor, why some make and perhaps sell only food and others make radios and stereos. Understanding economics may someday help solve problems like inflation.

1. In its broadest sense, economics is the study of

______(1) how prices go up
______(2) world trade
______(3) the cure for inflation
______(4) the value of money
______(5) the making and selling of goods and services

2. Inflation means that money's value is lowered. Inflation can happen because

______(1) more and more people want to buy gold
______(2) unskilled laborers are out of work
______(3) a country buys radios from another country
______(4) a great deal of money is in circulation
______(5) all of the above

3. If good drinking water becomes scarce because of pollution, its price will

______(1) go up
______(2) stay the same
______(3) go down
______(4) fall under government regulations
______(5) change, but we can't say how

4. We know that America went through a depression in the 1930s. Millions of people were out of work and millions of people stood in soup lines in order to get food to eat. From this passage we can infer that

______(1) another depression could never happen
______(2) one part of the depression was an upset in the balance between supply and demand
______(3) another depression would have no effect on world trade
______(4) the depression began because people were not working hard enough
______(5) another depression would keep money valuable

5. In order to solve economic problems like inflation we must first

______(1) understand economics
______(2) spend money
______(3) make money
______(4) buy food from a foreign country
______(5) be careful to use only what we need

Answers begin on page 42.

ECONOMICS PASSAGE 2

KEY WORDS

deduction—(noun) an amount that employers take out of their workers' paychecks for taxes, insurance or any other regular expenses

take-home pay—(noun) the amount of money a worker receives after deductions have been taken out of his or her paycheck

On Monday, Bob Franklin started working at the Fastgear Manufacturing Company. On Friday, he got his first paycheck. The check was made out for $100.85. The foreman had told Bob he'd be paid $140.00 a week. Maybe someone had made a mistake. But there was no mistake.

Bob's friend Luis showed him the list of deductions that had been taken from the $140.00.

"The company took out $17.10 to pay your federal income tax and $3.15 for your state tax," Luis explained. "This tax on income is one of the main ways we share the cost of running our government. Taxes pay for things like highways, public schools and national defense. Congress decides how much federal tax each of us has to pay. Then the Internal Revenue Service (I.R.S.) collects the taxes for the government. Our company withholds money from each of your checks and sends it to the I.R.S. That way you won't have to pay the whole tax at the end of the year. If the company takes out too much, you may get some money back. Before April 15, fill out a tax form and send it to the I.R.S. If you paid more than you owe for the year, you'll get a refund."

"I guess everyone should pay taxes," Bob said, "but what does this box marked F.I.C.A. mean?"

BOB FRANKLIN'S PAYCHECK AND STUB

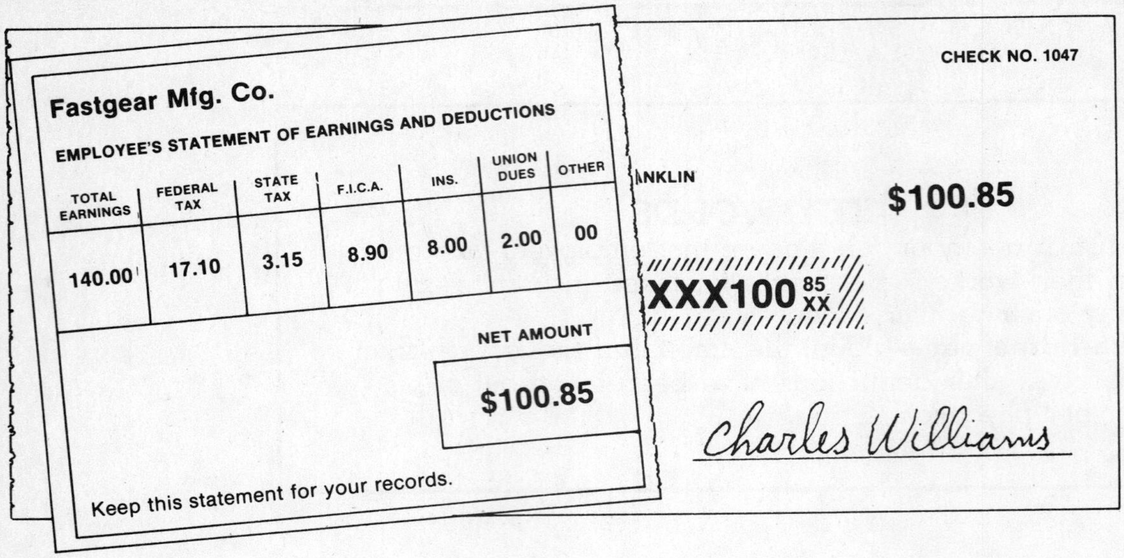

"Those letters stand for the Federal Insurance Contribution Act. That's the law that Congress used to set up the Social Security system. The federal government will use your $8.90 to help pay for the Social Security checks that senior citizens, and some other people who can't work, get each month. Because we're paying for it now, after we retire we'll get Social Security checks, too."

"Now look at those last two boxes. You paid $8.00 for health insurance and $2.00 for union dues. So after we subtract what you owed for taxes, Social Security, insurance and dues, your take-home pay is $100.85."

"Oh well," said Bob. "I didn't know I'd have so many bills to pay before I even got my paycheck."

6. What is the best title for this passage?
   ______(1) How the Government Robs Us
   ______(2) How to Keep an Eye on Your Foreman
   ______(3) Where Do Paycheck Deductions Go?
   ______(4) Why Taxes Keep Going Up
   ______(5) Social Security Is No Bargain

7. Choose the one which is *not* true. Federal income tax is a tax which

______(1) helps pay the cost of government
______(2) is used to help senior citizens each month
______(3) can be raised or lowered by Congress
______(4) all employees must pay
______(5) is based on the amount of money a person earns

8. Since the Internal Revenue Service collects taxes

______(1) it pays the army
______(2) it sends out Social Security checks
______(3) it has the power to raise or lower taxes
______(4) it is a part of our government
______(5) it is part of the accounting department at Fastgear Manufacturing Company

9. Which of the following would increase Bob's take-home pay?

______(1) Bob's landlady raises his rent
______(2) Bob uses his health insurance to pay for a visit to the doctor
______(3) Bob's union raises his union dues $.50
______(4) Bob's friend tells him he should save more money
______(5) Congress votes to lower the federal income tax

10. Based on Bob's experience with his first paycheck from the Fastgear Company, we can conclude that

______(1) companies support the work of government by paying the I.R.S.
______(2) citizens support the work of government when their employers withhold part of their salaries as income tax
______(3) unions support the work of government by deducting dues from workers' paychecks
______(4) the I.R.S. supports the work of government by paying citizens' income tax refunds
______(5) F.I.C.A. deductions support the work of government

Answers begin on page 42.

ECONOMICS PASSAGE 3

KEY WORDS

inflation—(noun) a condition of the economy when there is more money and credit than goods and services; prices go up

monopoly—(noun) a company that controls all of the making or selling of an item or service

recession—(noun) a condition of the economy when there is a slowing down of activity

Two weeks ago, Herb bought a loaf of bread for 55¢. This week the same kind of bread costs 65¢. In 1972 Rose bought a new car for about $3,700. When the 1981 models came out, she couldn't find a car she liked for less than $6,000. This problem of rising costs is called inflation—having to spend more and more money to buy the same goods.

Once inflation starts, it is hard to stop prices from climbing. If it costs a company more to make bread or cars, the company will charge store owners and car dealers more for those products. Then the store owners have to raise the prices they charge consumers.

Consumers are the people who buy the products. But most consumers are also workers. Workers are forced to ask for higher wages to pay for the things they need to buy. This is often part of the reason companies raise their prices again. The cycle starts over.

How does the inflation cycle start in the first place? There are many answers. Sometimes inflation is started by something that people have no control over. For example, a bad cold spell can ruin crops. Because the food is in short supply, it costs more. Other times a producer will raise the price of a product just to make more money. If no one else makes the same product, buyers have no choice. They have to pay the higher price.

When there is only one company that makes a product or provides a service, that company is called a monopoly. The telephone company is an example of a monopoly. Monopolies can raise prices as much as they like, until consumers run out of money to pay for the product, or until the government puts a limit on the price the company can charge.

Some people believe the government itself is the cause of inflation because it spends so much money. To make up for spending more money, the government collects more in taxes and fees from people and from companies. This, too, can boost inflation.

When inflation gets to a point where people can no longer afford high prices, people stop buying. When buying slows down, factories don't need to produce as much and the result is a recession. A recession is a period of slowed economic activity. People buy less, so less is produced and fewer workers are needed to make the products. Many people lose their jobs during a recession.

It is difficult to keep a country's economy moving well and avoid inflation. It is a problem that has troubled, and still troubles, the United States.

11. The main idea of this passage explains why

______(1) a recession is coming
______(2) inflation is such a hard problem to solve
______(3) the government should outlaw monopolies
______(4) inflation is a worldwide problem
______(5) workers are the cause of inflation

12. A recession happens when

______(1) inflation begins
______(2) there are no monopolies
______(3) consumers cause a depression
______(4) people buy fewer things and fewer things are produced
______(5) there is too much money

13. Choose the answer that describes a monopoly

______(1) at the neighborhood council party, both the Springfield Jogging Club and the Garden Club run hot dog booths
______(2) Jeanne starts a babysitting service to help parents find sitters. Eight of the ten teenagers in the area who babysit work for Jeanne's service
______(3) a wealthy family buys all the grocery stores in Las Vegas
______(4) Midway Airlines starts scheduling flights from New York City to Chicago
______(5) a Japanese company, Datsun, exports most of its cars to the United States

14. During the years shown on the chart, what can you guess about wages?

______(1) wages went up for some people
______(2) wages did not change
______(3) wages were high for everyone
______(4) wages were fair for everyone
______(5) wages went down for most workers

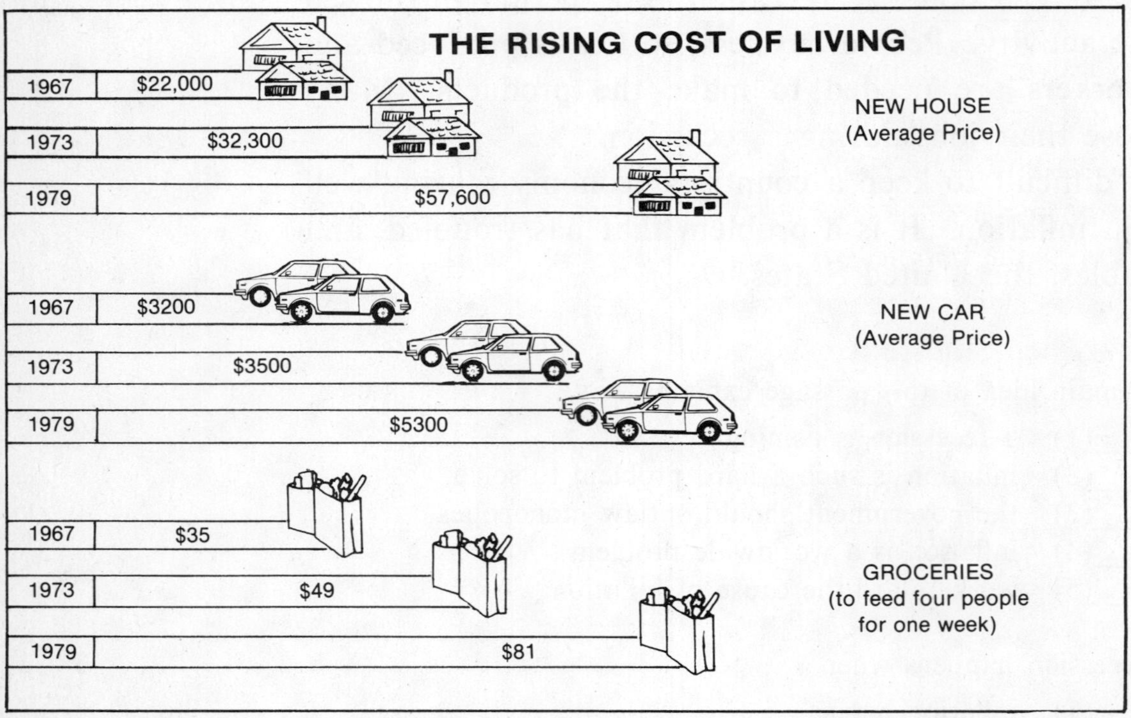

15. You can conclude from the passage that inflation

______(1) must always be present
______(2) is not related to the cost of living

______(3) helps to improve the standard of living
______(4) causes shortages of goods
______(5) is a problem that cannot be easily solved

Answers begin on page 42.

ECONOMICS PASSAGE 4

KEY WORDS

import—(noun) a product brought into a country from other nations
export—(noun) a product one nation sends to another nation
international trade—(noun) the exchange of goods and services between nations

The power of a nation is measured by more than the strength and size of its army. A nation's standing in today's world is measured by its economic muscle.

To remain strong, a country must provide all the goods and services its people need. It must also be able to sell goods and services needed by other nations. No nation is completely self-sufficient. All depend on other countries to provide some of the raw materials or products they need.

Products brought into one country from another country are called imports. For every item a nation imports, some money goes to another country.

Products that one nation sends to another nation are called exports. For every item a country exports, it receives money from another country.

The exchange of goods and services between nations is called international trade.

To decide whether a nation's economy is strong, economists look at the amount of money a country spends on imports and the amount of money that a country makes from its exports. The amount of money a country gets from exports along with the amount it spends on imports is called the balance of trade.

A nation is economically strong if the amount of money it makes from other nations is more than the amount it sends to other countries to buy goods. When the amount of goods imported is more than the amount of goods exported, the economy of a nation is weak.

If country X is exporting many products to country Y, but country Y isn't exporting any products to country X, there may be problems. A good example of this situation has occurred between the United States and Japan. These two countries are very good friends, but there are some tensions between them.

For years Japanese auto makers have built cars that get better gas mileage than American-made cars. This is because gasoline has always been very costly in Japan. Efforts were made long ago to come up with cars that get as much mileage as possible from each gallon of gasoline. The gas mileage chart on the next page shows that eight of the top ten cars in 1980 were Japanese-made.

In the 1970s when the price of gasoline went up sharply in the U.S., many Americans began buying Japanese cars. U.S. auto makers were still building big cars that used a lot of gasoline. By buying Japanese cars Americans could save money.

U.S. auto makers were out of luck. They couldn't sell their cars in this country and they couldn't export them to Japan, where gasoline is even more costly. There seemed to be no market for big cars that used lots of fuel. So the U.S. auto industry put pressure on the U.S. government to limit the number of Japanese cars that could be sold in the U.S. The sales of American cars had been hurt because of a better Japanese product.

Economists feel that a nation must try to have a balance between what it sells to other countries and what it buys from other countries if it is to survive as an independent power. In that way, nations are a lot like people. They should not spend more than they make.

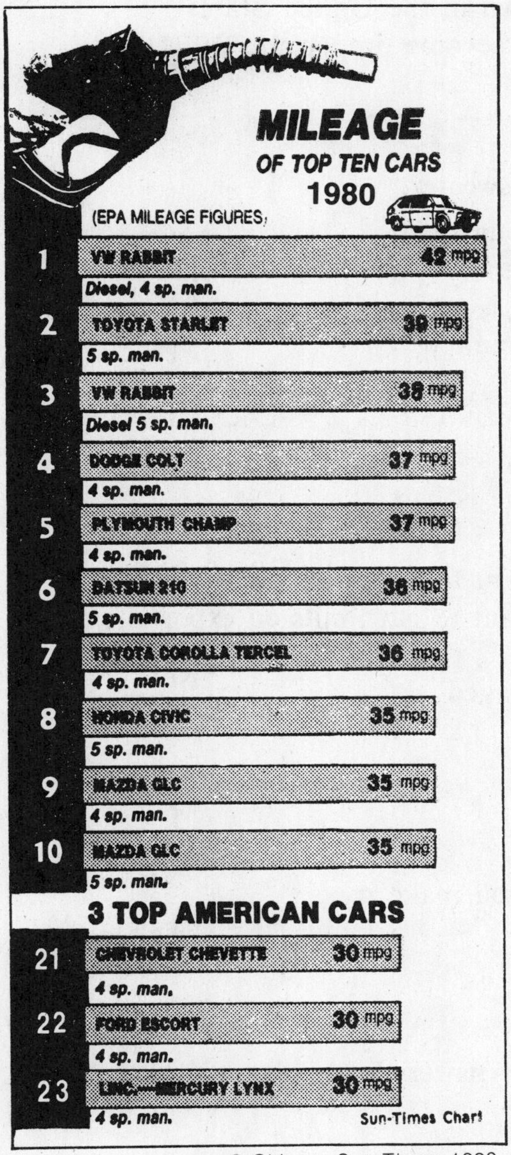

16. Balance of trade refers to

_____(1) the amount of goods a country imports

_____(2) the balance between the sale of Japanese cars and the sale of American cars

_____(3) the balance between money going out of the country and money coming in

_____(4) a nation that is self-sufficient

_____(5) the amount of international trade

17. Japanese cars have been successful in the United States because

______(1) people like imports
______(2) Japanese car advertising has been strong
______(3) the American car industry is smaller
______(4) gas prices have gone down in the United States
______(5) good gas mileage has become important in the United States

18. When an American buys an Italian sweater,

______(1) money comes into the country
______(2) the economy gets stronger
______(3) clothes prices go down
______(4) money goes out of the country
______(5) people get richer

19. If the United States' balance of trade is bad,

______(1) other countries are happy
______(2) the government might want to put limits on imports
______(3) the government might want to put limits on exports
______(4) prices are lower
______(5) more imports are encouraged

20. A strong economy depends on

______(1) lots of international trade
______(2) spending money before you make it
______(3) a strong army
______(4) a good balance of trade
______(5) lots of imports

Answers begin on page 43.

ECONOMICS PASSAGE 5

KEY WORDS

capitalism—(noun) an economic system in which certain persons or groups own land, factories and other means of producing goods; they compete against one another to earn a profit

capital goods—(noun) factories, tools and machines used to make things to sell

production—(noun) making things

communism—(noun) an economic and political system in which land, factories and other means of producing goods are owned in common

When people live together, they always find ways to get things they want and need. They find ways to trade with other people. All people need food, clothes and a place to live. In modern life, we also need services such as health care, education, transportation, electricity, running water and telephones. The whole system of making and delivering goods and services is called an economy or economic system. There are many kinds of economic systems.

Capitalism is the economic system of the United States. In a capitalist economy, individual people or corporations own capital goods such as factories, tools and machines. The people who own these capital goods are called capitalists. Capitalists use capital goods to make a wide range of products to sell for more than it costs to make them. The difference between the selling price and the cost of making a product is called a profit. Business owners can set whatever price they want for their products (though consumers can always decide not to buy if they don't like the prices).

Under capitalism, there is little government control of prices, production and delivery. To keep the system running, the government does try to keep any one company from making or selling all the products of one kind. For example, it won't let only one company sell all the gasoline.

Under this system, capitalists and consumers make big and little choices about what to buy and what to sell without government control. This is called the "free market." But, of course, in real life, economies do not work as clearly as this. The capitalist system and the free market are the ideas that the American economic system is based on.

Communism, another economic system, is based on *common* ownership of capital goods. Factories, machines and tools belong to all the people instead of to one person or one company. Things like furniture, clothes and bicycles still belong to the person who buys and uses them, however.

TWO DIFFERENT ECONOMIC IDEAS

CAPITALISM
In a capitalist system, individuals own factories, farms, machines and other means of producing goods.

COMMUNISM
In a communist system, all members of society share ownership of factories, farms, machines and other means of producing goods.

A German, Karl Marx, was the best known writer about the ideas of communism. He felt that people could get together to decide what the society should produce and how it should be shared. He thought people should work for the good of society and not for their own profit. He felt this would spread a nation's wealth in a fair way and overcome the problem of the "haves" and the "have-nots."

Capitalism and communism are very different economic systems or ideas. There are other economic systems that take some ideas from both of these. But no economy ever works exactly the way it is supposed to. People are always looking for better ways to run their economies. The perfect system has not yet been found.

21. What does the writer think is a basic difference between capitalism and communism?

______(1) who owns the factories and machines and decides how they are to be used
______(2) how much the government cares about the people
______(3) whether people own cars or bicycles
______(4) capitalism always works, but communism does not work
______(5) the writer thinks there is no difference between the two systems

22. Under capitalism what will be made and how much will be bought is decided by

______(1) giant computers owned by corporations
______(2) government rules
______(3) business owners and consumers
______(4) asking all the members of society to vote
______(5) economic ideas in books

23. The passage suggests that in a communist system

______(1) there are no very poor people
______(2) people cannot own their own television sets
______(3) capital goods are owned by a few people
______(4) everyone is rich
______(5) the government puts everyone in jail

24. The writer would agree with which of the following statements?

_____(1) people's needs cannot be served by communism
_____(2) people should try to understand different economic systems
_____(3) people should forget about the economy unless they own a factory
_____(4) people do not need government systems
_____(5) people cannot change society

25. Which of the following would not help a capitalist nation run smoothly?

_____(1) respect from other nations
_____(2) support from its own citizens
_____(3) jobs for all the workers who live in it
_____(4) ample food supplies
_____(5) one company which makes and sells all the cars

Answers begin on page 43.

ECONOMICS PASSAGE 6

KEY WORDS

barter—(noun) a system of trading goods and services without using money

currency—(noun) the money that a group of people uses; dollars, quarters and dimes are part of the currency of the U.S.

For as long as there have been people, there has been some plan for sharing work. In prehistoric times, men hunted to get meat for food. Women bore and raised children and gathered roots and berries to eat.

Later, people settled down into small communities. Some took up farming. New kinds of work came about. New kinds of goods and services started. With those new goods and services came a new class of workers. They were potters and tool-makers, weapon-makers and carpenters. Of course, there were medicine men and priests.

A farmer might trade grain for pottery. A potter might trade a bowl or jar he made for the services of the medicine man. A medicine man might heal someone's sickness in exchange for the services of a carpenter. Trading goods and services in this way is called barter. Barter made it possible for a person or a family to use many different kinds of goods and services. People were no longer limited to using only what they themselves could grow or make. But there were problems. Trading took a lot of time. Sometimes it took several trades to get what was needed.

In time, groups decided to pick some type of token to use as a form of money. They gave it a set value and used it in trade. The token was usually a rock or shell. It could be used within the community to buy goods and services. These tokens were the first money.

The tokens used as early money were worthless outside the small community. As trade grew between communities and nations, gold, silver and copper became the widely used tokens of trade.

Even this was a problem. The metals had to be checked and weighed each time a trade was made. The answer to this problem came when coins were made. Historians think that coins were first used in India around 3,000 years ago.

The use of paper money is fairly new. Government-backed paper money started in the American colonies in the late 1600s. In part this came about as a way to avoid paying taxes on English money. Several kinds of currency were in wide use after the Revolutionary War. In time, the dollar came to be the money unit of the U.S.

At one time the value of the dollar was set by the gold standard. This meant that each dollar was backed up by a set amount of gold that the government had in reserve. At another time, U.S. money was backed by silver. This meant that each dollar was based on a set amount of silver. Today, the dollar is backed by U.S. goods and services. Its value lies in our ability to produce goods and services wanted and needed both in America and in other nations.

Although people still barter and trade today, the use of money—both paper and coin—has made it easier for us to get the goods and services that we need.

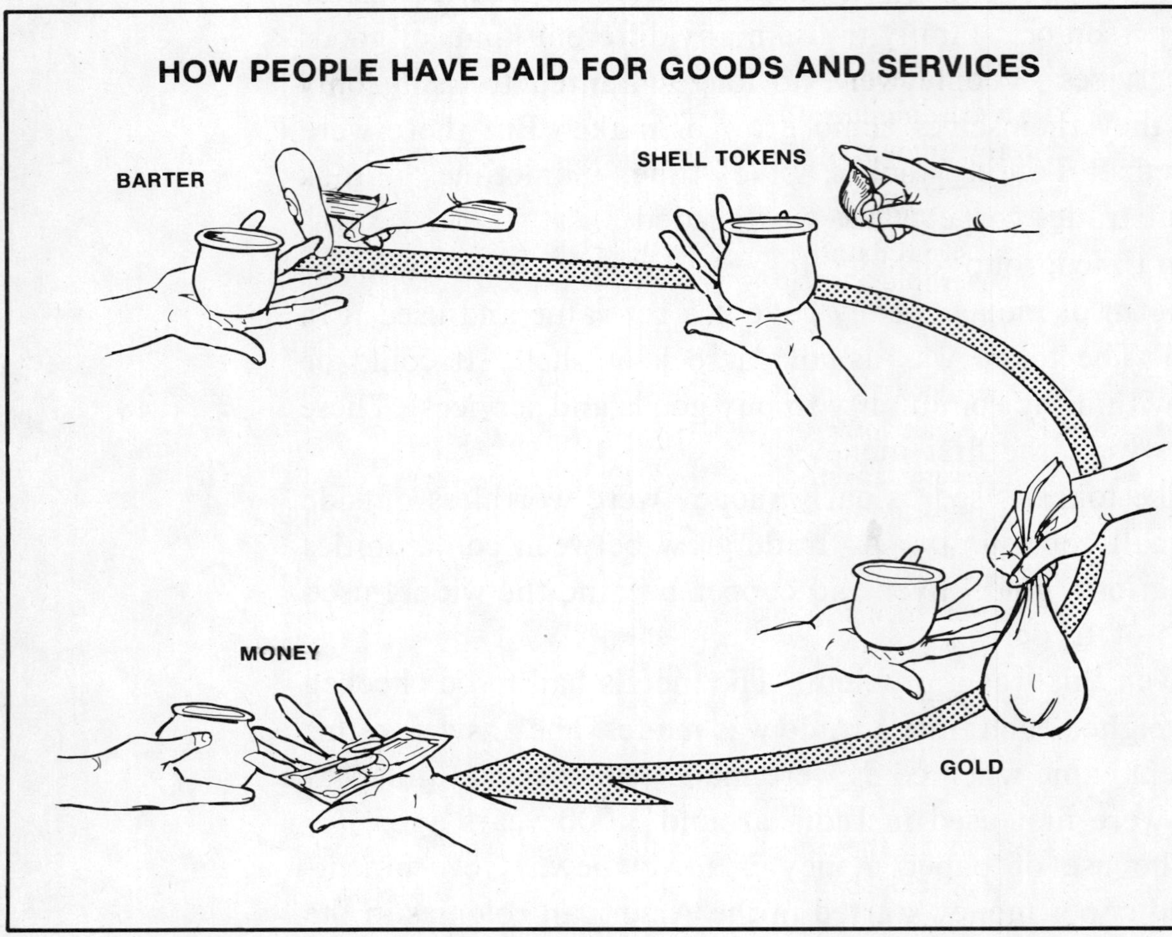

26. A good title for this passage is
    ______(1) The Development of Money
    ______(2) Sharing Work
    ______(3) Bartering through the Ages
    ______(4) The History of America
    ______(5) Gold, Silver and Copper

27. The biggest problem with using tokens was
    ______(1) tokens were so small that thousands were needed to pay for the services of a medicine man
    ______(2) carpenters did not want to use rocks or shells for purchasing goods

______(3) tokens could be lost easily
______(4) people did not want to give up bartering
______(5) tokens were worthless outside the community

28. If the U.S. dollar were backed by oil, then each dollar would be based on
______(1) a set amount of gold from the government reserves
______(2) a set amount of silver from the government reserves
______(3) any amount of goods and services from the American society
______(4) a set amount of oil from the government reserves
______(5) a set amount of gold, silver or copper from the government reserves

29. Because the writer tells us that paper money is backed by the government, we can infer that
______(1) a strong government will have a strong currency
______(2) a weak government will have a weak currency
______(3) an unstable government will have an unstable currency
______(4) governments and money affect each other
______(5) all of the above

30. The reason that the use of money grew from the practice of bartering was
______(1) to make the exchange of goods and services easier
______(2) to develop banks
______(3) to avoid taxes
______(4) so as not to use up all the world's shells
______(5) all of the above

Answers begin on page 44.

ANSWERS AND EXPLANATIONS—ECONOMICS

1. (**5**) is the best answer. It is the most complete answer. Every other answer is only a part of the study of economics.

2. (**4**) is the correct answer. (4) is the only reason for inflation that is given in the passage. Find this detail in the fourth from the last paragraph.

3. (**1**) is the correct answer because the law of supply and demand tells us that the value of a product goes up if it is scarce and many people want it. Everybody needs water.

4. (**2**) is the correct answer. The others are all false.

5. (**1**) is the only correct answer.

6. (**3**) is the correct answer. The other answers are opinions that aren't stated in the passage.

7. (**2**) is the correct answer. (1), (3), (4) and (5) are all listed in the passage as facts about the income tax. Social Security payments (F.I.C.A.) are given to senior citizens. They are, however, taken out of paychecks the same as is income tax.

8. (**4**) is the correct answer. Congress decides how high taxes will be and how much will be spent on the army. The Social Security Administration sends out Social Security checks.

9. (**5**) is the correct answer. This can be inferred from the information given in paragraph three. (1), (2), (3) and (4) would not mean that Bob would take home more money.

10. (**2**) is the best answer. We can conclude from the passage that it is working citizens, not companies (1), unions (3), the I.R.S. (4) or the F.I.C.A. (5) that pays for the work of the government.

11. (**2**) is the correct answer. The passage is mainly about the broad problem called inflation. It tells what it is and some of the reasons we have it.

12. (**4**) is the correct answer. The other answers are not true based on what is said in the passage. The Key Words tell us also that a recession is a slowing down of economic activity.

13. **(3)** is a monopoly because the family would be the only one that could sell groceries in Las Vegas. In (1), (2), (4) and (5) consumers could buy the products (hot dogs, babysitting, flights between New York and Chicago and cars) from more than one business.

14. **(1)** is the best answer. The writer tells you that all parts of the economy are related. The pattern of higher costs goes with higher wages for some people. Many working people, though, find that their wages don't rise as much or as fast as the cost of living.

15. **(5)** is the correct answer. None of the others is true.

16. **(3)** is the correct answer. The other answers are not true.

17. **(5)** is the correct answer. The Japanese were making cars that got good gas mileage before American companies thought they would be in demand.

18. **(4)** is the correct answer. Because money goes out of the country when people buy imports, there must be money coming into the country from exports to balance things out.

19. **(2)** is the correct answer. (1) is not true because other countries are affected in a bad way when the American economy weakens. Americans won't be able to afford to buy as many of their products. The other answers are also not true.

20. **(4)** is the correct answer. This is the best conclusion you can draw after reading the passage.

21. **(1)** is the best answer. Factories and machines are capital goods. The passage says that capital goods are owned by individuals or corporations under capitalism and that capital goods are owned by the whole society under communism.

22. **(3)** is the correct answer. The writer says that buyers and sellers control how much will be made and sold under capitalism.

23. **(1)** is the best answer. The author states that a communist system spreads a nation's wealth in a fair way and tries to overcome the problem of the "haves" and the "have-nots." This suggests that there are no very rich people or very poor people.

24. **(2)** is the best answer. None of the other answers can be supported by the passage. Although it does say that economies are never perfect, it does not say they cannot be changed.

25. **(5)** is the best answer. The writer says that a capitalist government would try to keep a company from selling all the products of one kind.

26. **(1)** is the correct answer. It is the broadest way of saying what the passage is about.

27. **(5)** is the correct answer. This detail is given in the passage. The other answers are not.

28. **(4)** is the correct answer. The writer explained what happened when the U.S. dollar was backed by gold and silver. We can apply this to what would happen if the U.S. dollar were backed by any other thing, including oil. The U.S. dollar might be backed by copper, diamonds or even wheat. Presently it is backed by U.S. goods and services.

29. **(5)** is the correct answer. All those inferences are correct once we have the fact that paper money is backed by the government.

30. **(1)** is the correct answer. (2) and (3) did happen, but they are not reasons for the growth of money.

UNIT II: GEOGRAPHY

Geography is the study of the earth's land, water and air. It includes how and where plants and animals live on the earth.

Directions: **The following passages cover topics in geography. Each one starts with one or more Key Words. The Key Words will give you an idea of what the passage is about. They are also used in the passage along with other words that might be new. You will be able to figure out the meanings of some new words as you read them in the passage. Look up any word that is new in the Glossary at the end of the book, or use a dictionary.**

After each passage, there are five reading skill questions to answer. Make a check (✓) next to the BEST answer for each question. Check your work using the Answers and Explanations section at the end of the unit. It starts on page 65.

GEOGRAPHY PASSAGE 1

KEY WORDS

topography—(noun) the physical features on the surface of land—lakes, mountains, roads and valleys, for example

climate—(noun) the average weather conditions of a place—temperature, rainfall, humidity and wind conditions, for example

The physical features of the land on which we live help to shape the way we live. A person who lives in the jungles of a country in Africa leads a very different life from a person who lives in the mountains of China. Living near the city of New Orleans, Louisiana is very different from living near Chicago, Illinois. This is because these four places have different topographies and different climates. These differences have led to different customs and styles of living. Geography is the study of these differences.

Through the study of differences in topography and climate we come to understand why a person who lives near a desert would have trouble raising cattle and why someone living high on a snow-covered mountain would not be wise to try to grow wheat. An area's climate and topography affect what the land can produce, what kinds of buildings are built and how people travel and live.

Natural resources also affect people's lives. Natural resources are the products of nature. They can include minerals in the soil, metals in the ground, forests, bodies of water and many other things that are valuable to people. Natural resources influence what we eat, how we are clothed and what types of materials we use to make buildings, tools and other things. The natural resources of different areas also play a part in how different countries or regions interact with each other.

In addition to looking at natural resources and physical features of the earth and how they are formed and used, geography studies the societies that have grown up in different places. It studies how different societies, or groups of people who live together and share the same customs and values, interact with other societies. Scientists feel that geographic features play an important role in human behavior.

We know that each society finds ways to survive on Earth. People in different parts of the world have taken on different ways of life. Geography helps us to explain and understand these differences. At the same time, we see that with radio, TV and easy travel between countries, many societies have grown more alike. The study of these changes and how they affect people is also part of geography.

All of this means that geography is much more than the study of places on Earth. It is also the study of people finding ways to live in the widely differing topographies and climates on Earth.

1. In its broadest sense, geography is the study of
   ______(1) people who live in deserts and jungles
   ______(2) the relationship between governments and natural resources
   ______(3) the relationship between climate and topography
   ______(4) groups of people with the same customs
   ______(5) the relationships between people and the earth

2. Geographers are concerned with all of the following EXCEPT
   ______(1) the type of buildings people live in
   ______(2) where minerals and metals can be found
   ______(3) the way people travel
   ______(4) how to make money for oil companies
   ______(5) how people get their food

3. People who live in very cold climates
   ______(1) are no different from people who live in hot climates
   ______(2) are always uncomfortable and hungry
   ______(3) are all alike
   ______(4) develop ways to stay warm and comfortable
   ______(5) would rather live in a warm climate

4. The passage implies that
   ______(1) the earth and its features affect many aspects of human life
   ______(2) there is only one reason to study geography
   ______(3) lakes are good for swimming and fishing
   ______(4) geography is concerned only with the study of places
   ______(5) natural resources do not affect the way countries deal with each other

5. The conclusion of this passage is that
   ______(1) people who live in the desert should not try to grow crops
   ______(2) studying geography will make you want to move to a different climate
   ______(3) geography is less important than other sciences
   ______(4) geography is a broad and complex field
   ______(5) societies will always be different

Answers begin on page 65.

GEOGRAPHY PASSAGE 2

KEY WORDS

cartographer—(noun) a person who makes and studies maps

latitude—(noun) distance measured in degrees on the surface of the earth from east to west; lines of latitude are called parallels

longitude—(noun) distance measured in degrees on the surface of the earth from north to south; lines of longitude are called meridians

Have you ever made a map? If a friend wanted to come visit you, you might draw a map to show how to get to your house. On the map you could show the streets near yours, the park to pass on the way and the empty lot across from your house.

People have made maps for thousands of years. They made maps even before they wrote. The oldest known map was made around 2300 B.C. in the Middle East. This map was drawn on wet clay. Other early maps were drawn on bark, bone or hide. They most likely showed hunting trails and where to find water.

A map is a picture of a place. Most maps are drawn to scale. This means that a certain distance on the map always stands for a certain real distance. Suppose you made a map of your house and the scale of your map is one-fourth inch to one foot. This is written ¼:1 foot. This means that what takes up one foot in your house is shown to take up one-fourth inch on your map. If your living room is really 12 feet long, it will be shown as three inches long on your map. Most maps of countries have a scale of one inch to 100 or 1,000 miles. A map of the world in a book will have an even smaller scale: 1:10,000 miles. Most maps will say what the scale is. Also, most maps will have a compass. The compass is an arrow that shows which way north is on the map.

A map can be used to show many different kinds of places. You may have seen maps of your city and state. There are also maps of oceans, star maps and maps of the moon. Some maps show mountains, plains, valleys and hills. There are maps of highways and maps that show the amounts of rainfall different places get in one year. Some maps show different places and what languages people speak there. Others show what religion the people of an area believe in.

People who make maps are called cartographers. Cartographers have developed a system of lines called latitude and longitude to help them map the earth. Lines of longitude are called meridians. They are drawn around the earth from north to south, through the North and South Poles. Lines of latitude are called parallels. They are drawn around the earth from east to west. The lines of latitude and longitude are numbered. They are used to measure distances and to say where a city or a forest or a lake is.

HOW CARTOGRAPHERS MAP THE EARTH

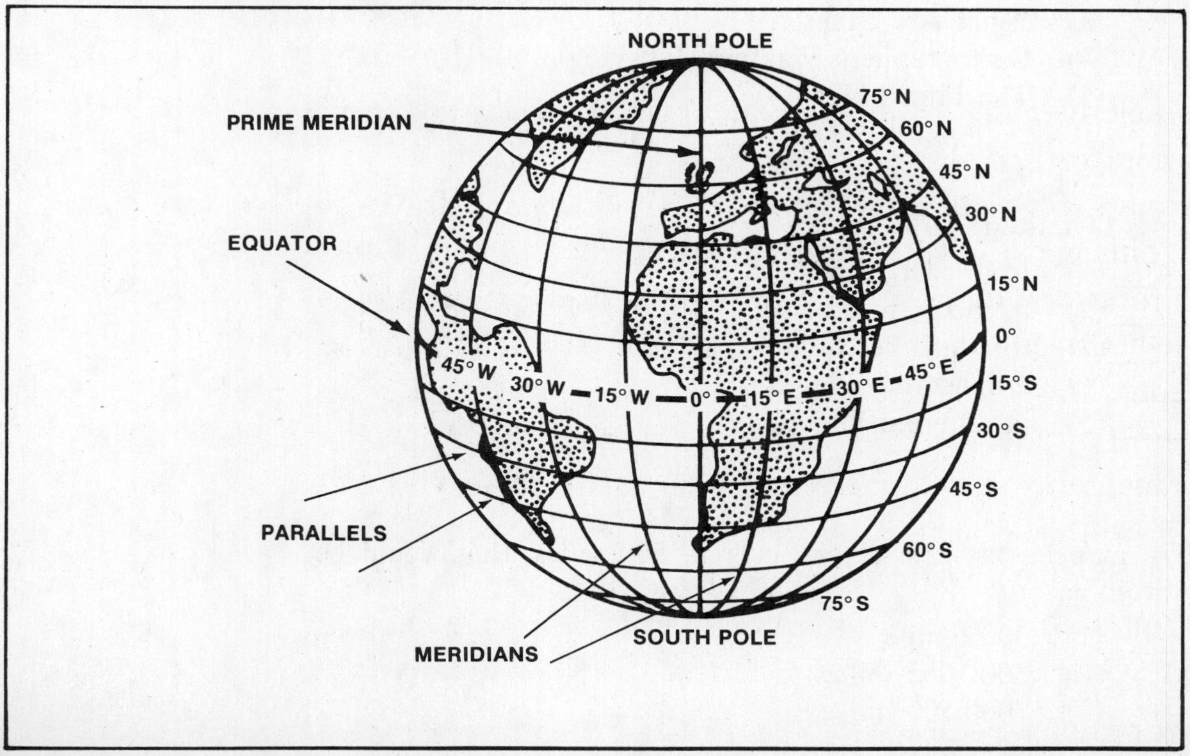

The line of latitude that goes around the middle of the earth is called the equator. The equator is called 0° latitude. On the map, the first line north of the equator is 15° north latitude. The first line south of the equator is 15° south latitude.

The lines of longitude also have numbers. The 0° line of longitude is called the Prime Meridian. It passes through Greenwich, England, and parts of Spain and Africa. On the map here, the first line to the west of this 0° line is 15° west longitude. The second line to the west is 30° west longitude. Most of the United States is between 60° and 120° west longitude, and between 30° and 45° north latitude.

Maps are very useful in our daily lives. They help us to know where other places are and where we are in relation to other places. By looking at maps we can learn many things about the different parts of the world.

---

6. A good title for this passage would be

______(1) How to Use a Compass
______(2) Understanding Latitude and Longitude
______(3) What Are Maps?
______(4) Cartographers Making Maps
______(5) The First Maps

7. Lines of latitude go

______(1) from east to west
______(2) from north to south
______(3) through the equator
______(4) around the poles
______(5) in different directions

8. If a map has a scale of one inch to 500 miles, that would be written as

______(1) 500:1 mile
______(2) 500:1000 miles
______(3) 1000:500 miles

______(4) 1:500 miles
______(5) 1/5:500 miles

9. The weather is very hot near the equator. If a woman lives at 15° north latitude, what would we know about the place where she lives?

______(1) it is very cold
______(2) it is very hot
______(3) it is near England
______(4) it is west of the 0° line of longitude
______(5) it is somewhere in the United States

10. After reading the passage, you can conclude that

______(1) maps are a new tool being used by today's cartographers
______(2) maps of oceans, lakes and rivers cannot be drawn
______(3) only cartographers can make maps
______(4) cartographers don't really need to use latitude and longitude
______(5) maps can show many facts about places

Answers begin on page 65.

GEOGRAPHY PASSAGE 3

KEY WORDS

province—(noun) one of 10 regions of Canada; each is like a U.S. state
Parliament—(noun) a group of appointed and elected people who make Canada's laws
prime minister—(noun) head of the government of Canada

The United States is a big country, but it has an even bigger neighbor to the north—Canada. Canada covers nearly four million square miles and is the second largest country in the world.

Just as the U.S. is divided into 50 states, Canada is divided into 10 provinces. The far northeastern part is made up of many islands. To the southeast, near the Great Lakes, are the cities of Toronto, Quebec, Montreal and the capital city of Ottawa. Two-thirds of all Canadians live in this Great Lakes region. Even though it is a larger country, Canada has only one-ninth as many people as the United States.

Canada is rich in natural resources. In the central plains wheat is plentiful. To the north are huge forests which supply wood as well as asbestos (a material used to make things fireproof), fish, furs, copper, nickel, lead, silver and zinc.

CANADA

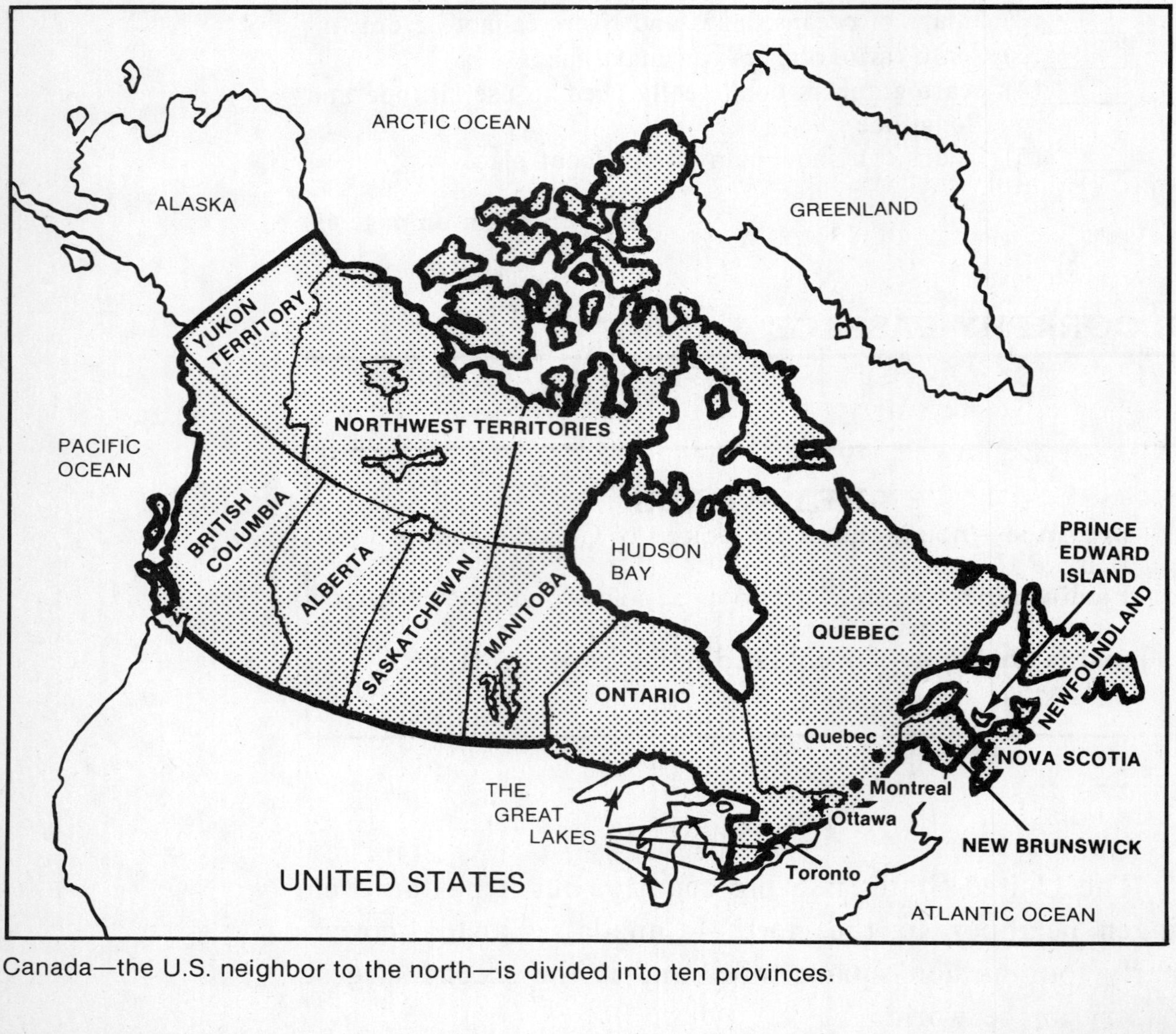

Canada—the U.S. neighbor to the north—is divided into ten provinces.

Like the U.S., Canada is so large that the weather can be very different from one part to another. Far from the icy north forests are warmer areas in the central and eastern parts.

Canada has a parliamentary system of government. The Canadian Parliament consists of two houses—the Senate and the House of Commons. Senators are appointed by the government and members of the House of Commons are elected by the people. The head of the country is the prime minister. The prime minister is also the leader of the strongest political party in the Parliament.

Because Canada is such a large country, people of different regions have different interests and different ideas. They even have different languages. While most of the people in Canada speak English, many who live in the province of Quebec speak French.

A heated dispute within the country involves the French language and customs of Quebec. Though Quebec was founded by the French, some people want Quebec to give up the ties to her past and become like the rest of English-speaking Canada. Others believe Quebec should become a separate country. It is a complicated problem. Canada's people and leaders are working to solve it.

Canada and the United States are neighbors as well as long-time friends. Each buys the other's products and allows easy travel across the shared borders. Both value the goal of world peace through friendship and understanding.

11. One way in which Canada is different from the United States is

______(1) its people have a low standard of living
______(2) it is made up of 50 provinces
______(3) it has rich natural resources
______(4) it has many kinds of weather
______(5) it has fewer people

12. Canada's land area is
______(1) the largest of any nation in the world
______(2) about four million square miles
______(3) smaller than the United States
______(4) 300,000 acres
______(5) larger than the Soviet Union

13. Few people live in the far north forests of Canada because
______(1) it is a good place to grow wheat
______(2) it does not have a local government
______(3) the prime minister will not allow it to be settled
______(4) it is very cold
______(5) it has few natural resources

14. From what the passage says about the dispute in Canada between those who speak French and those who speak English, you might say that
______(1) this will become a problem with the U.S.
______(2) the larger a country is, the more chance for differences between its people
______(3) they are not interested in solving the problem
______(4) it is really a simple problem
______(5) people who live in a large country will never get along

15. The conclusion of the last paragraph is that Canada
______(1) is near the United States
______(2) exports many goods
______(3) is in the western hemisphere
______(4) is a peaceful nation
______(5) has much in common with the United States

Answers begin on page 65.

GEOGRAPHY PASSAGE 4

KEY WORDS

mestizo—(noun) a person of mixed Indian and Spanish background

peso—(noun) the Mexican unit of money

While the English were settling the area that was to become the United States, the Spanish were landing farther south in what is now Mexico.

When they came in the early 1500s, the Spanish found an Indian society that had built great cities, set up its own calendar, invented a way to count, and developed its own form of writing. The Spanish conquered the Indians, but the Indian culture did not die. The Spanish and the Indian ways of life grew together to form a Mexican culture.

Mexico is about three times the size of the state of Texas. Nearly 70 million people live in Mexico. Almost 90 percent of these people are mestizo—a mixture of Indian and Spanish blood. Spanish is the official language, but many Indian languages are also spoken. The unit of money used in Mexico is called the peso.

Mexico is a country that in some ways is very different from the United States. Its language and many of its customs are different from those of most Americans. Mexico's government is in some ways like the U.S. government. There are 31 states. Each has its own governor and law-making body. There is a president at the head of the country.

Mexico is a land of deserts and rugged mountains. The climate in most of Mexico is very hot, and in some areas Mexico is very rainy. The geography and weather have made farming very difficult. Yet Mexico grows corn, beans, wheat, coffee, cotton, sugar cane, oranges and tobacco. The country's main industries are mining, oil-drilling, fishing and the manufacture of cigars and cigarettes. Because of the world's great need for oil, Mexico's oil reserves are expected to be very important to the country and the world in the years ahead.

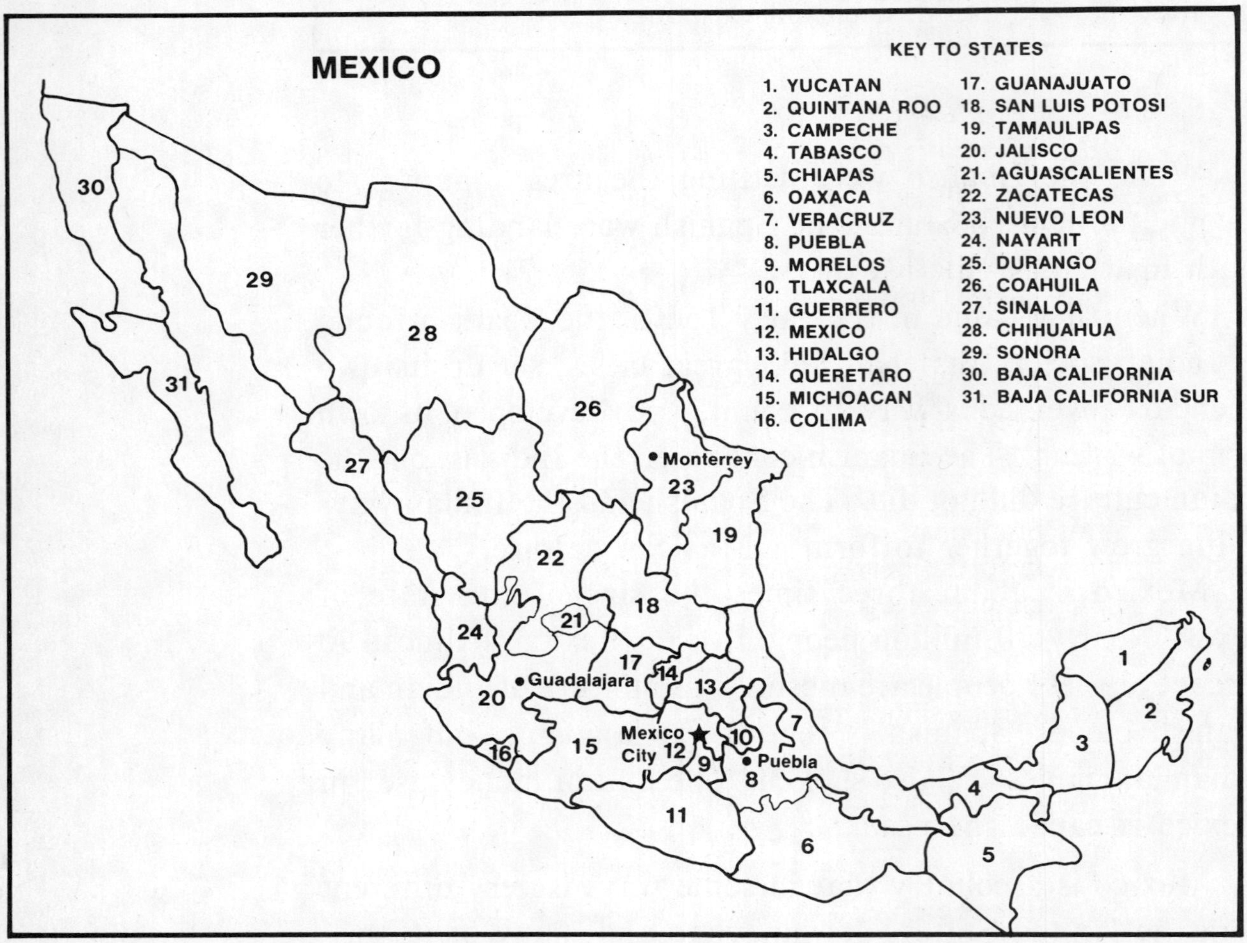

Although Mexican industry and farming have improved in recent years, the country still has a large problem finding food, housing, education and jobs for its ever-growing population. Nearly half of its people are under the age of 15, and the population is growing faster than homes and schools can be built. Poverty is a serious problem facing Mexico.

Officials hope that the large supplies of oil that have been found in Mexico will one day be the key to solving some of these problems.

16. A good title for the passage is
    ______(1) The History of Mexico
    ______(2) Mexican Society—Then and Now
    ______(3) The Importance of Mexican Oil Reserves
    ______(4) Facts about Mexico—Our Neighbor to the South
    ______(5) The Spanish Conquest of Mexico

17. All of the following are facts about Mexico EXCEPT
    ______(1) Mexico is three times the size of Texas
    ______(2) Mexico has the same unit of money as the U.S.
    ______(3) the government is headed by a president
    ______(4) poverty is a serious problem in Mexico
    ______(5) nearly 70 million people live in Mexico

18. Mexico's newly found oil can best be used to
    ______(1) keep other countries from spending money in Mexico
    ______(2) keep down the price of gasoline in the United States
    ______(3) improve Mexico's economy and help solve some of its problems
    ______(4) keep the population from growing
    ______(5) change the government

19. The passage tells us that the weather and geography make farming in Mexico difficult. From this, we would think that
    ______(1) many Mexicans are descendants of Indians
    ______(2) a large part of the population is very young
    ______(3) Mexico only grows corn and wheat
    ______(4) Mexico must use its farmland well if it is to feed all its people
    ______(5) Mexico has many minerals

20. After reading the passage you can conclude that Mexico is a country
    ______(1) whose federal government has two branches
    ______(2) with no capital city
    ______(3) with a Spanish and Indian culture
    ______(4) with a vast corn belt
    ______(5) in which few people live in villages

Answers begin on page 66.

GEOGRAPHY PASSAGE 5

KEY WORD

Orient—(noun) the area of the world we call the Far East; the eastern countries of Asia including China, Korea, Japan and the Philippines

The Orient, or the Far East, is one of the oldest and most interesting parts of the world. Covering much of the continent of Asia and nearby islands, the Orient is made up of the countries of China, Korea, Japan, the Philippines and several other countries. During the 1980s the two countries of the Orient that are most important to the government and people of the U.S. are China and Japan.

China stands out because of its size, population, age, culture, history and politics. With 3.7 million square miles of land, China is the third largest country on Earth. Only the Soviet Union and Canada are larger.

China has the largest population of any country. Close to one billion people live within its borders. Ninety-four percent of these are the Han people. Of the rest, 56 million are other ethnic groups or minorities. China's minorities equal the populations of New York, Illinois, Ohio and California.

In 1981 China celebrated the year of the rooster. This was the Chinese year 4679. Throughout China's long history, politics has been important. The Communist Party, under Mao Tse-tung, came to power in 1949 after a long revolution. Since then its members have ruled the country. During 1966-1969, China's great Cultural Revolution took place. China turned inward and had little to do with the U.S. Its government put tight controls on the people.

Since the revolution, China has found ways to feed,

clothe, house and educate its millions of citizens for the first time in history. Even so, some still say that the government has too much control over people's lives.

Relations between China and the U.S. have never been easy. In recent years, though, the two countries have opened their doors to each other. In 1978 the U.S. officially recognized or accepted China's communist government. Today more and more Chinese products are available in the U.S., especially clothing and handmade goods. The U.S., in return, sells China the machinery that it needs to build up its industries. People of each country can travel more freely to the other.

A SIZE AND POPULATION COMPARISON

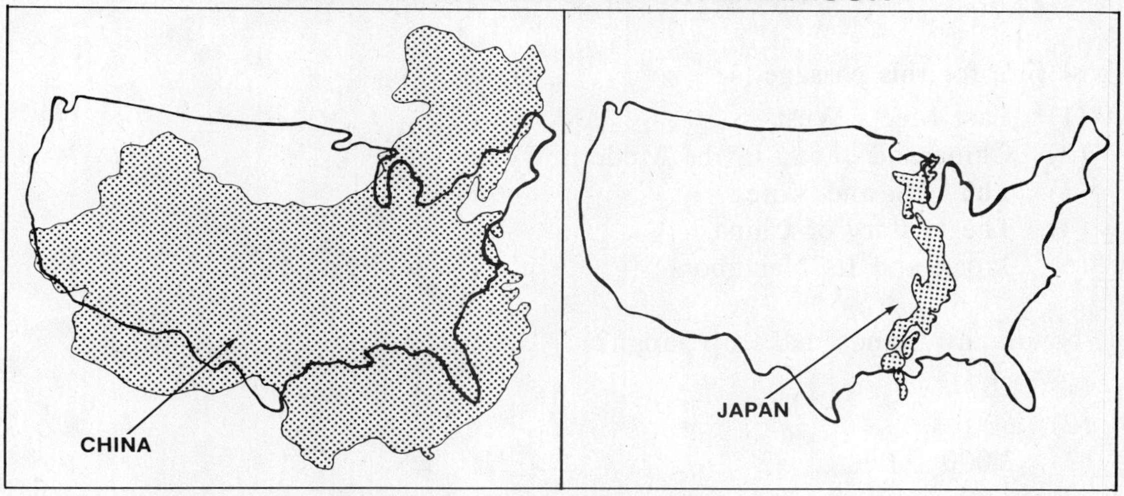

The above maps compare the land area of China and of Japan to that of the United States. Although China is not much larger than the U.S., it has 4½ times the population. Japan, on the other hand, is much smaller than the U.S. but has over half as many people.

Japan differs from China in many ways. Its population of 115 million seems small compared with China's 960 million. But China has a land area 26 times that of Japan. Japan is made up of more than 3,000 islands. People live on only about 500 of these. Like England, Japan is a monarchy. This means that its leader is an emperor, queen or king. Although Japan has an emperor, the people elect a parliament to govern the nation and make its laws.

Unlike China, Japan has been very successful in making and selling all kinds of things. Before World War II, Japan had little to do with Western countries. But today Japanese cars, computers, cameras, radios and televisions are very popular in the U.S. and throughout the world.

Because the population of China is so large, the U.S. and other countries think that China could someday again be a very powerful nation. Right now, China is a country with few modern factories. The Chinese government is trying hard to change that. On the other hand, Japan has some of the most modern and productive industries in the world. Both China and Japan are important to the government and people of the U.S.

21. The best title for this passage is

_____(1) East Meets West
_____(2) China and Japan in the Modern World
_____(3) The U.S. and Korea
_____(4) The History of China
_____(5) Japan and Its Neighbors

22. About how many islands make up Japan?

_____(1) 26
_____(2) 500
_____(3) 3,000
_____(4) 7,000
_____(5) several million

23. If someone told you "I was born in Japan," you could be sure the person

_____(1) had Japanese parents
_____(2) was born in a city
_____(3) had voted in a parliamentary election
_____(4) was born on an island
_____(5) is an industrial worker

24. Years ago a Chinese leader said that his country could give up millions of soldiers and not miss them. He wanted the U.S. to think that

_____(1) America should share food with his crowded nation

______(2) America should beware of a war with such a huge nation
______(3) China should be recognized for its accomplishments
______(4) communism has been good for China
______(5) the Chinese do not value life

25. We can conclude from this passage that
______(1) once industry is developed, China's population will decrease
______(2) Japan may change its government to be more like China's
______(3) China and the U.S. will never have smooth relations because of China's communist government
______(4) Korea, Viet Nam and Thailand no longer have relations with the U.S.
______(5) countries of the Orient have been and will continue to be important to the U.S.

Answers begin on page 66.

GEOGRAPHY PASSAGE 6

KEY WORDS

population—(noun) the total number of people living in a place
life expectancy—(noun) the number of years a person is likely to live

One of the biggest problems facing the world today is the population explosion. The population of the world is growing at a faster and faster rate. If the population keeps growing this way we will have problems finding enough food for all the world's people.

The graph on the next page shows how population growth has speeded up. It took about four million years for the population of the earth to reach 800 million people. Over these years population growth was very slow. Later, the number of people started growing much faster. It took only 200 more years for the population to reach 4.1 billion people. By the year 2014 the population is expected to be 8.2 billion people.

WORLD POPULATION GROWTH

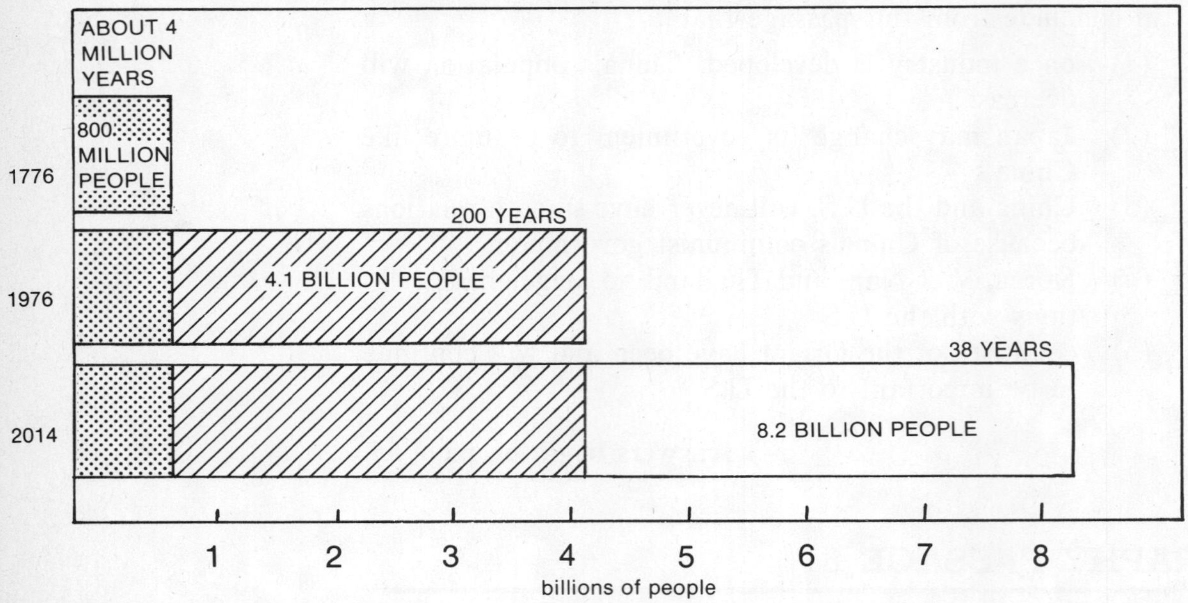

An important cause of this rapid population growth is improved medicine and nutrition. Long ago many young children died from disease or because they didn't have enough food to eat. In some places only one child out of five lived to be five years old. In many countries these problems have been almost wiped out.

People also live longer than they used to. Life expectancy means the number of years a person is likely to live. Hundreds of years ago life expectancy was about 40 years. Now in the United States, life expectancy is about 72 years.

One reason the population increase is so dangerous is that the countries that are already poor are the ones that have the fastest population growth. India, Africa and Latin America are areas that have especially high rates of population growth. Even today many people in these countries are badly undernourished.

There are two ways that the population problem might be solved. The first is the use of birth control to lower the number of children born. In developed countries like the U.S., Canada, Japan and the countries of western Europe, birth control has already lowered the population growth a great deal. In less developed areas such as India and Latin America birth control methods are often not understood or are not available. In many countries, especially in Latin America, people are against birth control for religious reasons.

The other way to help ease the population problem is to find ways to produce more food. Mexico, Holland and Japan are countries that have been very successful in producing large amounts of food on small amounts of land. Japan's population has gone up 134% in the last 100 years. During this time Japan's food production has increased by 300%. Scientists are beginning to come up with high-yield types of corn and wheat in which each plant produces more grain than in the past.

The growing population could cause problems all over the world if something isn't done about it soon. To solve the problems we will have to think carefully about the limits of the world's resources.

26. The writer thinks that the population problem

_____(1) is getting worse and must be solved
_____(2) can be blamed on Japan
_____(3) will be solved in the near future
_____(4) has been blown up to be worse than it is
_____(5) may destroy America within the next generation

27. In the year 2014, the world's population probably will be

_____(1) smaller than now
_____(2) the same as now
_____(3) about 8.2 billion
_____(4) three times as big as now
_____(5) 16.4 billion

28. Suppose that all nations stopped their population growth and produced food at Japan's rate. One result would be
______(1) world control by Japan
______(2) a decrease in world population
______(3) very little food per person
______(4) not much land per person
______(5) more food per person

29. The writer doesn't say it directly, but you can tell that
______(1) India, Africa and Latin America will soon have world power
______(2) there is less violence in the world now than there used to be
______(3) birth control will not catch on in large countries
______(4) fewer children die now than in earlier times
______(5) people are not living as long as they used to

30. The last paragraph concludes that
______(1) time will solve man's problems
______(2) a war will end the population problem
______(3) the earth is doomed
______(4) atomic bombs are a greater threat than the population problem
______(5) people must act quickly to solve the population problem

Answers begin on page 66.

ANSWERS AND EXPLANATIONS—GEOGRAPHY

1. **(5)** is the correct answer. The other answers are parts of geography but do not describe geography in its broadest sense.

2. **(4)** is the best answer, although a geographer who works for an oil company might have this as one of his or her concerns.

3. **(4)** is the correct answer. The other answers are not true or not necessarily true. You have to apply what you read about the role of climate to come up with the right answer.

4. **(1)** is the correct answer. None of the other choices should be made after carefully reading what the passage says.

5. **(4)** is the correct answer. The passage gives a wide range of topics that are studied in geography.

6. **(3)** is the best title. The others are only supporting details of the main idea. They would not be good titles.

7. **(1)** is the correct answer. All the others are false.

8. **(4)** is correct. The third paragraph explains how scale is shown.

9. **(2)** is correct. The passage tells us that the 15° latitudes, either north or south, are close to the equator. Therefore, 15° north latitude would probably have a similar climate.

10. **(5)** is correct. The passage shows that (1), (2), (3) or (4) cannot be true.

11. **(5)** is the correct answer. The choice of answers checks your understanding of some main points made in the passage. (1) and (2) are false. (3) and (4) are facts that are also true of the U.S.

12. **(2)** is the correct answer. This detail is in the first paragraph.

13. **(4)** is the correct answer. See the second and fourth paragraphs.

14. **(2)** is the correct answer. It is the only choice that is a good inference from what is said in the passage.

15. **(5)** is the correct answer. The other answers are true but are not the conclusion of the last paragraph.

16. **(4)** is the best answer. It is broad enough to cover the many ideas of the passage. (1), (2), (3) and (5) are not broad enough to cover everything stated in the passage.

17. **(2)** is the correct answer. One of the facts given about Mexico is that its unit of money is called the peso. All the other choices are true facts about Mexico.

18. **(3)** is the correct answer. This would be of most use to the greatest number of Mexican people.

19. **(4)** is the correct answer. This is the only answer that follows from the fact that farming is difficult in Mexico.

20. **(3)** is the correct answer. This is a conclusion which can be reached from several statements in the passage. All other choices are false.

21. **(2)** is the correct answer. The other titles have meanings either too broad or too narrow to fit what the passage tells us about China and Japan.

22. **(3)** is the correct answer. This detail is in the sixth paragraph. We are also told that people live on only 500 of the 3,000 islands.

23. **(4)** is the correct answer. We read that Japan is made up completely of islands. From this we know that anyone born in Japan must have been born on an island. The other answers may or may not be true.

24. **(2)** is the best answer. America would be badly outnumbered in a war with China. In those days, relations between the two countries were not good because of political differences.

25. **(5)** is the correct answer. It is the only conclusion that is based on what the passage says.

26. **(1)** is correct. The first paragraph says that if the problem gets worse, we will not be able to feed the world's people. (5) is wrong because the writer never says that this will happen.

27. **(3)** is correct. Find the information in paragraph two and in the chart.

28. **(5)** is correct. If population growth stopped, the world population would not decrease, but would be about the same as now. Since more food would be produced, the same number of people would have more food per person.

29. **(4)** is correct. Paragraph three talks about how many children in the past died from disease or from not enough food. Since in many countries these problems have almost disappeared, you can guess that fewer children die now than in earlier times.

30. **(5)** is correct. In the last paragraph the writer says that something must be done soon about the population problem.

UNIT III: POLITICAL SCIENCE

Political science is the study of how governments form and work. It may look at nations, states, cities, towns or any other place where people live together.

Directions: The next passages cover topics from political science. Each one starts with one or more Key Words. The Key Words will give you an idea of what the passage is about. They are used in the passage along with other words that might be new. Look up any new word in the Glossary at the end of the book, or use a dictionary. You will be able to figure out the meaning of some words as you read them in the passage. Also, be sure to study any pictures or graphs that go with the readings.

There are five reading skill questions to answer after each passage. Make a check mark (✓) next to the BEST answer for each question. Be sure to read all five choices first. Check your work using the Answers and Explanations section at the end of this unit. It starts on page 91.

POLITICAL SCIENCE PASSAGE 1

KEY WORD

federalism—(noun) the sharing of power between states and a central government

Today's American government began more than 200 years ago. By looking at the events of that time we can see why our government works the way it does. We can see how the power of the federal government grew as the states saw the need for a strong central body.

On July 4, 1776, men from the 13 British colonies met in Philadelphia to sign the Declaration of Independence. The Declaration of Independence created 13 independent states. These states joined together to fight a common enemy in a war we now call the Revolutionary War.

After the Revolutionary War, men from each of the states met to lay out a long-term plan for working together.

The Articles of Confederation, adopted by the states on July 9, 1779, laid out a plan for a weak central government with most powers going to the states. The states wanted a central government strong enough to protect the new country, but not so strong that it took away their own powers. They felt that the states should keep making their own laws.

It soon became clear that what was needed was a plan by which states would share power with the central government. This sharing of power between states and the central government is called federalism. The central government is called a federal government.

The plan worked well enough to get the country through the Revolutionary War. But after the war, problems began. Conflicts between the states and the weak federal government began. The central government had the power to tax the states but had no power to make sure they paid. The central government also had no power to control trade between the 13 states. It could not stop a rebellion in the states if one started. It had no power to settle differences between the states.

In 1787 representatives of the states met again to change the Articles of Confederation. They ended up writing a whole new plan—the Constitution. The new Constitution called for a much stronger central government. The central government alone had the power to declare war. Alone, it could control trade between the states. It was the only body that could coin or make money. It ran the post office. These powers came to be called exclusive powers of the federal government.

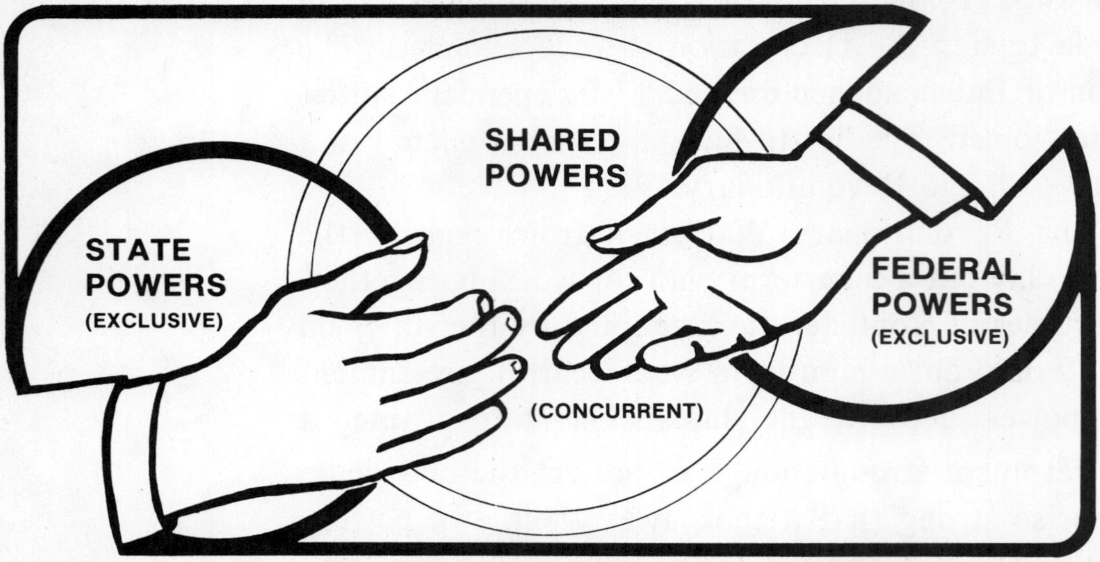

The U.S. Constitution provides for exclusive and concurrent powers.

Other powers were shared by the states, with each state keeping power over most matters within its borders. These powers became exclusive state powers. Still other powers—concurrent powers—are shared by both federal and state governments.

The Constitution has remained the plan for how the American government works. It makes a strong central government. At the same time, it protects the rights of each state.

1. Which question deals with the main idea of this passage?
   ______(1) What happened just before the Revolutionary War?
   ______(2) What does having a strong government mean?
   ______(3) How did power come to be shared between the central government and its member states?
   ______(4) How are laws made under federalism?
   ______(5) How did the 13 colonies rebel against Britain?

2. One of the exclusive powers of the central government of the U.S. is the power to
   ______(1) coin money
   ______(2) make laws
   ______(3) hold elections
   ______(4) tax people
   ______(5) enforce laws

3. If the central government had no power, there would be
______(1) a lack of freedom for each state
______(2) no national trade agreements with other countries
______(3) no schools or colleges
______(4) a lack of banks and loan companies
______(5) no private corporations

4. If there were no concurrent powers,
______(1) we would never go to war
______(2) only one level of government would have the power to tax
______(3) there would be many revolutions in our country
______(4) no one would obey laws
______(5) some states would not have mail delivery

5. You can conclude that the author believes
______(1) the writers of the Constitution failed to plan a good government
______(2) the Articles of Confederation were better than the Constitution
______(3) state governments should have more power
______(4) federalism is a workable system for the U.S.
______(5) America has a weak central government

Answers begin on page 91.

POLITICAL SCIENCE PASSAGE 2

KEY WORDS

separation of powers—(noun) the division of duties and powers of the federal government into three branches: the executive, legislative and judicial

checks and balances—(noun) the system set up to make sure that each branch of the federal government does what it is supposed to; each branch watches and checks actions of the other branches

"That government is best which governs least."
Over the years, most Americans have believed this.

They have wanted a government that could protect its people and help make the country rich and strong. But they have not wanted the government to tell people how to run their lives. Even though Americans elect the government, they have feared that even elected people will sometimes use their power badly or try to take more power.

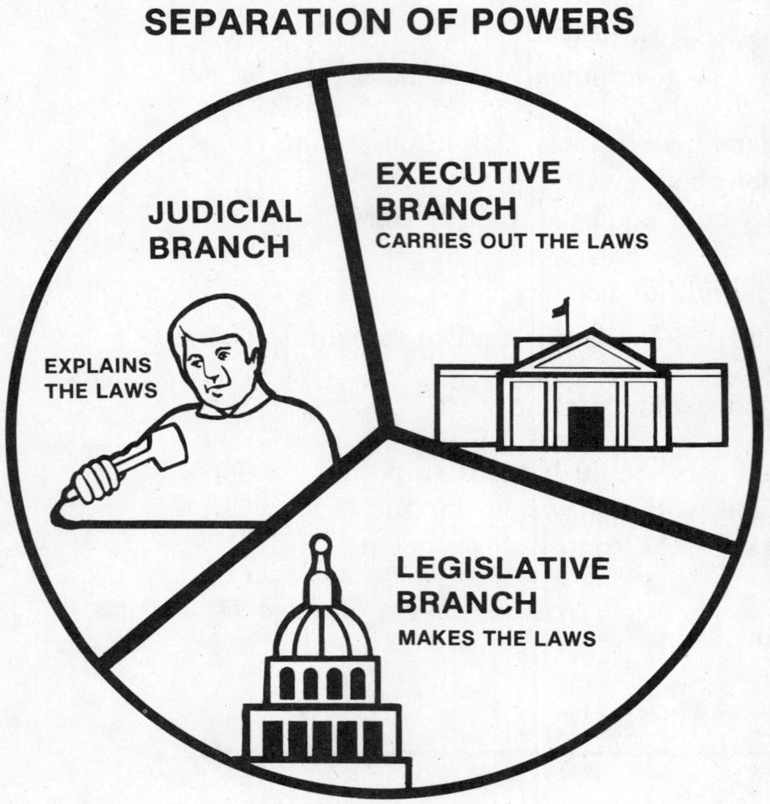

The U.S. Constitution does three important things to keep the government from getting too powerful. First, it says what the government may and may not do. Second, the Constitution divides power between the federal government and the state governments. Third, it divides power among three branches of government—legislative, executive and judicial. This division is called separation of powers.

The legislative branch makes laws. It is called Congress. Members of Congress are elected by the people of their home states. This keeps the power of Congress separate from the power of the other branches.

The executive branch enforces the laws and sees that things like government housing programs, the defense of the country and the government budget work well. The president is in charge of the executive branch. He gets help from the people who head departments such as the State Department, the Department of Health and Human Services and the Defense Department.

The judicial branch is our system of courts. The courts judge cases to decide on guilt and to settle disagreements. Sometimes the courts must explain laws. This happens when two sides in a case have different ideas about what a law or a part of the Constitution really means.

To make sure that one branch of the government doesn't get out of line or disobey the Constitution, we have the system called <u>checks and balances.</u> This allows each branch to serve as a "watch dog" over the others.

Here's how it works. The president may veto or turn down a bill passed by Congress. The Senate, part of Congress, may ratify or veto some of the president's actions, such

CHECKS AND BALANCES

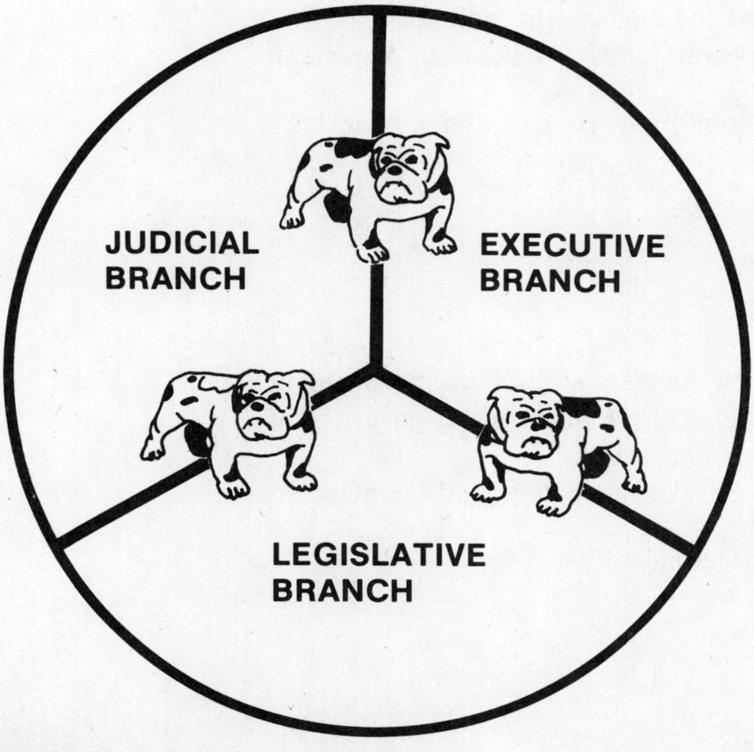

Each branch of the federal government acts as a "watchdog" over the other two branches.

as treaties and people he appoints. The courts may look at decisions that both Congress and the president make. If the courts say a law or action is not allowed by the Constitution, the president or Congress has to go along. Congress can impeach government officials or judges if it thinks they have done something illegal. This means the official would be accused of a crime and put on trial. If found guilty, the official could then be removed from office.

This form of government has lasted some 200 years. In the last 50 years the federal government has tried to deal with many problems the Constitution writers never dreamed of—poverty, pollution, inflation and energy. We citizens must understand how the Constitution limits what the government can do about such problems. And we must decide how much power we want our government to have to solve problems.

6. The writer thinks that

______(1) Americans dislike too much government power
______(2) there are too many laws in America and few are kept
______(3) there is little need for checks and balances
______(4) separation of powers has weakened American government
______(5) justice has been done in every case under America's judicial branch

7. Separation of powers means

______(1) dividing power between state and federal government
______(2) dividing power among three branches of government
______(3) having a written constitution
______(4) dividing power between elected and nonelected officials
______(5) not interfering in people's lives

8. Suppose that the U.S. president began taking illegal powers. What would protect the American system?

_____(1) the courts could fine him up to $10,000
_____(2) a plan to fire him could be written for state governors to act on
_____(3) nothing could be done until the next election
_____(4) Congress could impeach him—if convicted, he could be removed from office
_____(5) people could call for a new election to be held at once

9. The checks and balances system is needed because

_____(1) it provides jobs for more people
_____(2) it helps balance the federal budget
_____(3) people depend on it to explain laws
_____(4) people in government might take too much power unless there is a way to control them
_____(5) the president relies on it for advice

10. The last paragraph says that

_____(1) the American system is no good
_____(2) the American system of government can solve all problems
_____(3) people should think carefully and possibly change how much power the government has
_____(4) government power is unlimited
_____(5) limits on government mean the government can't do anything about problems

Answers begin on page 91.

POLITICAL SCIENCE PASSAGE 3

KEY WORDS

civil right—(noun) a right that belongs to a person because he or she is a member of a state or nation

amendment—(noun) a change; especially a change in the Constitution

discrimination—(noun) treating a group of people in an illegal or unfair way

segregation—(noun) the forced separation of races in schools, neighborhoods, jobs or public places

Civil rights are rights that belong to a person because he or she is a citizen, a member of a state or nation. One civil right is the right to vote. Another is the right to own, buy or sell property. We also have the civil right to use the courts and the legal system.

Civil rights are granted by the Constitution and by laws of Congress. Groups who have been denied their rights have struggled to change the Constitution to protect their rights.

There are 26 amendments or changes already added to the Constitution. The Fourteenth Amendment makes it clear that black people are citizens. The Fifteenth Amendment protects black citizens' right to vote. Women received the right to vote under the Nineteenth Amendment and 18-year-olds under the Twenty-sixth Amendment. Many people want the Equal Rights Amendment (E.R.A.) to be added to the Constitution. It would forbid discrimination on the basis of sex.

Besides amendments, federal laws have also been passed to insure people's rights. The first of these was the Civil Rights Act of 1866. It said that black people had the same rights as white people.

The Civil Rights Act of 1875 tried to end segregation, the forced separation of the races. At that time there were laws to keep black and white people apart on trains, in restaurants and in schools. These were called Jim Crow laws and they lasted for nearly 100 years. One reason Jim Crow laws survived was that the 1875 act was soon declared unconstitutional by the Supreme Court. The court said that acts such as refusing to serve black persons were legal because they were private acts. Having separate schools, toilets and train sections was legal as long as these areas were the same for both races. This came to be known as the idea of "separate but equal." Not until 1954 did the court decide that separating the races was not right, fair or equal.

The Civil Rights Act of 1957 gave the federal government the job of protecting the civil rights of its citizens. It was seen that this job could not be left in the hands of state and local governments. The law allowed people to file civil suits in federal courts to protect their right to vote. It also promised fair housing and schooling. The Commission on Civil Rights was a special group set up to enforce these rules.

The Civil Rights Act of 1960 gave the U.S. Department of Justice the power to carry out the 1957 law. Under this act, federal judges could stop acts of discrimination in the states.

Public marches and sit-ins in the early 1960s led to the 1964 Civil Rights Act. This act was broader than any before. It set up funds and advisors to help solve racial problems at a local level. It gave more protection to black voters. It outlawed discrimination in hiring and in labor union laws. Further, it suggested holding back federal money from state programs not obeying the Civil Rights Act of 1964. Finally, it gave federal money to public schools that opened their doors to students of all races.

In 1968 Martin Luther King, Jr., was killed. This led to the passing of another civil rights act to protect civil rights workers. It was also meant to control riots or violence that sometimes came with protests.

Thousands marched in the 1960s to demand equal rights for black Americans.

In spite of the many federal laws, enforcement of civil rights is still a problem. Even today, bad feelings and acts of discrimination exist.

11. A good title for this passage would be
    ______(1) Civil Rights in the United States
    ______(2) Public School Segregation
    ______(3) The Commission on Civil Rights
    ______(4) Voting Rights for Black Citizens
    ______(5) The Constitutional Amendments

12. The first federal civil rights act in 1866
    ______(1) amended the Constitution
    ______(2) said black people had the same rights as white people
    ______(3) destroyed the Jim Crow laws
    ______(4) gave citizens of all races the right to vote
    ______(5) protected civil rights workers

13. The passage says that civil rights are rights of every citizen. If so, why have some people had to struggle for them?
    ______(1) leaders were busy working on problems more basic than civil rights
    ______(2) not all people deserve rights
    ______(3) people's beliefs and behavior are not easily changed, even by law
    ______(4) it is too dangerous to grant new rights to those who have not had them
    ______(5) the Constitution and amendments were not understood by people

14. Which of these statements about the Civil Rights Act of 1957 is probably true?
    ______(1) it made black people citizens
    ______(2) the courts soon found it to be unconstitutional
    ______(3) there was a lack of power to carry it out completely
    ______(4) it worked well to end discrimination in hiring
    ______(5) it completely ended discrimination in voting

15. The writer concludes with the thought that enforcement of civil rights is still a problem. We could also conclude that
    ______(1) no real progress has been made by laws, acts and constitutional amendments
    ______(2) civil rights will never again be a problem in America
    ______(3) some civil rights laws harmed the working of the government
    ______(4) most Americans support civil rights, and laws are all that are needed
    ______(5) the gains made came because people were willing to fight for their beliefs

Answers begin on page 91.

POLITICAL SCIENCE PASSAGE 4

KEY WORDS

law—(noun) a rule for behavior or action made and enforced by some authority or power

inalienable right—(noun) something to which people have a just claim and which cannot be taken away

legislature—(noun) a group of people who have been given the power and authority to make laws

"All men are created equal and endowed by their Creator with certain inalienable rights." Those words, written by Thomas Jefferson more than 200 years ago in the Declaration of Independence, are the building blocks of American law. Laws serve to protect the rights of all citizens as much as is possible.

Inalienable rights are rights which cannot be taken away. Such rights, according to Jefferson, include "life, liberty and the pursuit of happiness." Sometimes the rights of one person conflict with the rights of another. In such a case it is the duty of the courts of law to decide where the rights of one person begin and the rights of another end.

The highest law in the land is what is stated in the Constitution. The Constitution spells out, in general terms, the rights of government and of citizens. It outlines what kinds of laws can be made.

Other laws are made by legislative bodies like Congress, state legislatures or city and town councils. These laws are called statutory laws. Statutory laws protect society from harmful actions of its members. The law that makes murder a crime and the law that sets a 55-mile-per-hour speed limit on a highway are both statutory laws.

Statutory laws must be based on the Constitution. A statutory law that violates the Constitution is illegal and cannot be enforced. Such a law is called unconstitutional. For example, the Constitution says no government can set up an official religion. That means a city council cannot pass a law that makes all its citizens go to church on Sunday. If a city should pass such a law, it would be unconstitutional.

The duty of deciding what is constitutional and what is unconstitutional belongs to the courts. The Constitution gives the courts power to interpret both the Constitution and all statutory laws.

While courts cannot make laws, their rulings that explain the Constitution and other laws become part of what is called common law. Common law is applied in cases for which there is no clear-cut constitutional or statutory law.

Statutory law is made by Congress or other lawmakers. Common law is based on past court cases. Both types of law must follow the guidelines of the U.S. Constitution.

The courts also are called upon to settle disputes between individuals or businesses. This area of law is called civil law. One of the most common matters covered in civil law is divorce. Civil law also covers cases in which a person claims to have been harmed by the lawful actions of another person. Such a case could involve a patient who claims his doctor failed to give him proper care. Another case could involve a worker who says her employer failed to treat her fairly.

In all cases, it is the duty of the law to protect the rights of the individual while keeping peace in society. To fulfill this duty a complex system of law serves us at many different levels.

16. The writer's purpose is to
    ______(1) show that man is evil
    ______(2) explain how laws can be changed
    ______(3) tell about different kinds of law
    ______(4) question the need for laws
    ______(5) suggest needed laws

17. Legislative bodies like Congress and state legislatures make
    ______(1) statutory laws
    ______(2) common laws
    ______(3) court rulings
    ______(4) constitutional rulings
    ______(5) religious laws

18. Which kind of case would not be found in a civil court?
    ______(1) legal separation
    ______(2) disagreement over the settlement of a will
    ______(3) murder in the first degree
    ______(4) a landlord trying to make a tenant move out for making too much noise
    ______(5) an argument about how to divide property after a divorce

19. If a citizen breaks a law that has been called unconstitutional, he
    ______(1) will be put in jail
    ______(2) cannot legally be punished
    ______(3) is no better than a criminal
    ______(4) does not understand the purpose of laws
    ______(5) loses his right to have a lawyer

20. From this passage, you can conclude that the purpose of laws is to
   ______(1) settle disputes between individuals or businesses
   ______(2) keep religion from being practiced unconstitutionally
   ______(3) protect the courts
   ______(4) assume the people are innocent until they are proved guilty
   ______(5) balance the rights of each person with the good of all members of society

Answers begin on page 92.

POLITICAL SCIENCE PASSAGE 5

KEY WORDS

due process of law—(noun) the correct and legal way that an arrest and a trial must be carried out

double jeopardy—(noun) being put on trial twice for the same crime

If a person is arrested, the police have to "read him his rights." What are these rights? What other rights does a person have if he or she is accused of a crime? Where do these rights come from?

The Fifth, Sixth and Eighth Amendments to the U.S. Constitution protect a person accused of a crime. The writers of the Constitution felt that police, prosecutors and judges might deny the rights of an accused person in an effort to solve a crime or to punish someone. For this reason certain rights and protections were added to the U.S. Constitution.

One of the provisions of the Fifth Amendment is the right to remain silent. This means that you do not have to confess to a crime, and you do not have to testify or answer questions against yourself in court. This protects people from being beaten or tricked into a confession. The police must tell an accused person of this right.

The Fifth Amendment also guarantees due process of law. This means that in the course of an arrest and trial every step must follow legal rules. For serious crimes a group of people called a grand jury must meet to hear the facts of the case. They must decide if a crime has actually been committed. The grand jury must also decide if there is enough reason for a particular person to be accused of the crime. Then a regular jury hears the case and decides the guilt or innocence of the accused person.

The Fifth Amendment forbids double jeopardy. This means that a person can be tried only once for a crime. If a person is accused and tried by a jury and found innocent, he or she can never be tried again for the same charge. Double jeopardy does not apply to different charges based on the same crime.

The Sixth Amendment attempts to insure a fair trial. It says that an accused person has a right to a trial by jury. It also says that the trial must follow soon after the person has been accused. Finally, the Sixth Amendment says that the trial must be public. The accused person must be told of the charges and be able to see and question the people who are witnesses against him. The government must help the accused person by allowing him to have a lawyer. It must even provide one free of charge if the person accused can't pay for one. The police must tell the accused person of this right to have a lawyer. And the government must help the accused person defend himself by helping to find witnesses for the defense—even those who don't want to testify.

The Eighth Amendment says that bail or bond money cannot be set too high. It also says that the punishment for a crime cannot be "cruel or unusual." This forbids punishments like chopping off hands. It can also protect prisoners from bad treatment in jail. Being in prison is supposed to be punishment enough.

All of these rights have sometimes been denied to people who were too powerless to demand them. But people who know the Constitution can use the Fifth, Sixth and Eighth Amendments to fight for their rights.

21. What would be the best title for this passage?
 ______(1) The U.S. Constitution
 ______(2) Amendments to the U.S. Constitution
 ______(3) The Rights of the Police
 ______(4) The Rights of Accused Persons
 ______(5) The Right to Remain Silent

22. A person may not be tried
 ______(1) if not a citizen
 ______(2) more than once on the same charge
 ______(3) until of legal age
 ______(4) for two different charges based on the same act
 ______(5) unless there is proof of guilt

23. Which of these is FALSE?
 ______(1) you do not have to be a witness against yourself
 ______(2) you have to be a witness for your friend, even if you are scared
 ______(3) the courts can't use witnesses who keep themselves hidden
 ______(4) you don't get a trial by jury if the judge thinks the case is too serious
 ______(5) the government will get you a lawyer if you can't pay for one

24. Police must tell an accused person of his right to a lawyer. What could possibly happen if they don't do this?
 ______(1) the person would go directly to jail and never get a trial
 ______(2) no witnesses would ever be found
 ______(3) the person might go free, even if he or she is guilty, because a right was denied
 ______(4) the person might not get a jury trial
 ______(5) other people might tell him his rights later

25. The writer seems to think that
_____(1) the Constitution does not give accused people enough rights
_____(2) the Constitution gives accused people too many rights
_____(3) police might sometimes try to deny accused people their rights
_____(4) all Americans understand their rights well
_____(5) the police never tell people their rights

Answers begin on page 92.

POLITICAL SCIENCE PASSAGE 6

KEY WORDS

representative democracy—(noun) a government in which the citizens elect people to speak or act for them
elector—(noun) a person who is chosen to elect the president and vice-president of the United States
popular vote—(noun) the total vote of all the people in the country
electoral vote—(noun) the total vote of the 538 electors

Our country is a representative democracy. This means that we, the people, elect other people to do most of the work of government. We give power to our elected representatives.

The people we elect to Congress are not our only representatives. The president and vice-president are also elected to represent us, to carry out the wishes of the people. However, the way we elect them is rather confusing. We don't vote for them directly, even though it seems that way on election day. When we vote for a candidate for president, we are really voting for that candidate's electors from our state. They are the ones who really cast the vote for our candidate.

How did this come about? The majority of the men who wrote the Constitution thought that the average voter couldn't choose a president wisely. So the Constitution stated that we would vote for electors instead. Electors are people chosen just to elect someone. The idea was that the electors would be wiser than the average voter and would make a wiser choice of president. They promise in advance to vote for one candidate or another. This is why voting machines and ballots almost always have the names of the candidates for president and vice-president, not the names of the electors.

Each state has as many electors as it has representatives and senators in Congress. There are 435 representatives, and 100 senators. Washington, D.C. has 3 electors though it is not a state and has no voting representatives or senators. So there are 538 electors in all. Together they are known as the electoral college. The vote of the electoral college may differ from the popular vote, however, due to the winner-take-all rule for each state. The winner-take-all rule says that the candidate who gets the majority of the popular vote within each state gets all of that state's electoral votes. This means that even if the candidate got only 51% of all the votes, he or she will get 100% of the electoral votes. Then the electoral votes from all the states are added up.

To be elected president, a candidate must win a majority of electoral votes—270 or more. If no candidate receives a majority, the House of Representatives elects the president, and the Senate elects the vice-president.

The electoral system is not perfect. A candidate may try to win in just enough large states to get 270 electoral votes. And remember, the candidate can win all the state's electoral votes by winning only the smallest majority of the state's popular votes. He can ignore most of the smaller states because they have few electoral votes. It is possible, though not likely, that a candidate could get a majority of electoral votes even though his opponent had more votes from the people.

TOTAL NUMBER OF ELECTORS FROM EACH STATE*

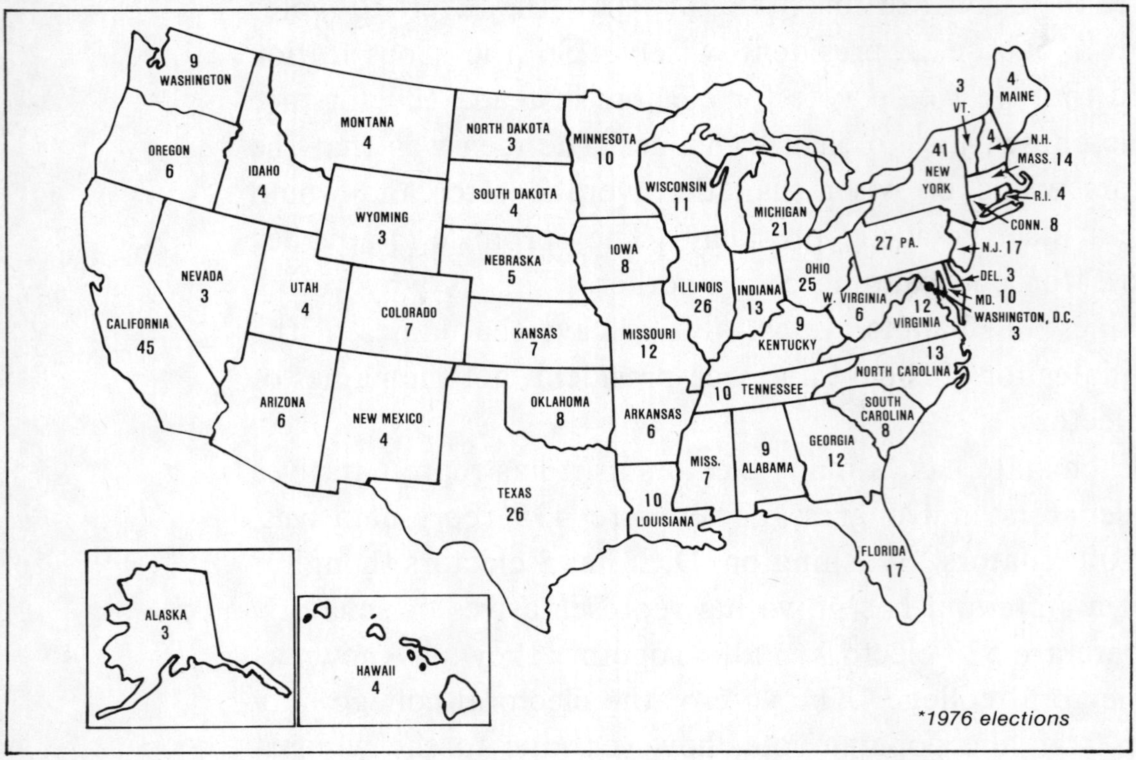

*1976 elections

Some people say that we should change the electoral college system to a direct popular vote for the president and vice-president. So far, not many people seem to think this is worth worrying about. What do you think?

26. The main purpose of this passage is to
    ______(1) describe the constitutional convention
    ______(2) discuss how Congress works
    ______(3) explain how the president is elected
    ______(4) report some unusual election results
    ______(5) explain the meaning of democracy

27. If one candidate does not get a majority of votes in the electoral college, the president is elected by
    ______(1) a new election
    ______(2) the House of Representatives
    ______(3) the Senate
    ______(4) a special convention
    ______(5) state legislatures

28. Which of the following might have too much influence under the electoral college system?

_____(1) a minority group from Montana
_____(2) a state with a lot of people, such as New York
_____(3) a large corporation
_____(4) a group of civil rights workers in Virginia
_____(5) a farmer's union in Missouri

"Whew! Can't We Find Some Other Route?"

From *The Herblock Gallery* (Simon & Schuster, 1968)

29. What is the cartoonist saying about the electoral college?

_____(1) it is like an ancient monster and should be replaced
_____(2) it is a powerful monster that gets rid of bad presidential candidates
_____(3) it's the best system we can find, even if it's not perfect

______(4) it isn't really worth worrying about
______(5) those who want to change this system are like monsters

30. Which statement expresses the author's view of the electoral college?
______(1) the American people do not know enough to elect a president directly
______(2) the founding fathers didn't know anything about the people
______(3) the founding fathers wanted power for themselves
______(4) there are some problems with the electoral system and perhaps we should change it
______(5) the electoral system is the only way to elect a president

Answers begin on page 92.

ANSWERS AND EXPLANATIONS—POLITICAL SCIENCE

1. **(3)** is the best answer. All of the passage deals with the growth of federalism, the system for sharing power between the central government and its member states.

2. **(1)** is the correct answer. The other choices are powers of government at national, state and local levels.

3. **(2)** is the best answer. Only our central government can make agreements between the U.S. and other countries.

4. **(2)** is the best answer. All the power to tax could have been given to either the central or state governments. We have no way of knowing if any of the other things would happen.

5. **(4)** is the best answer. The writer is not critical of the system or any part of it, as the other choices imply.

6. **(1)** is the best answer. The opening quote and the statement at the end of the passage express this.

7. **(2)** is the correct answer. It is defined in the passage.

8. **(4)** is the only correct answer under the Constitution.

9. **(4)** is the correct answer. The purpose of the checks and balances system is to allow one branch of government to check the work of another branch. The system maintains a balance of power between the three branches.

10. **(3)** is the correct answer. The last paragraph says the government has worked for some 200 years but has limits on what it can do about problems. In thinking about changing this, people should decide how much power they want to give the government.

11. **(1)** is the best answer. The others are all details that support the main idea.

12. **(2)** is the correct answer. Civil rights acts were passed in 1866, 1875, 1957, 1960 and 1964. The first made it clearer that black citizens had the same rights as white citizens.

13. **(3)** is the best answer. None of the other choices is a good general reason that could account for the problem.

14. **(3)** is the correct answer. The passage says the Civil Rights Act of 1960 gave the Department of Justice power to carry out the 1957 act. The 1957 act was not enough.

15. **(5)** is the best answer. History shows that change requires people who are willing to work for better conditions. History shows that these people must often go against strong feelings of others.

16. **(3)** is the correct answer. Most of this passage discusses different types of law, such as constitutional, statutory, common and civil law.

17. **(1)** is the correct answer. Find this detail in paragraph four.

18. **(3)** is the correct answer. The law that makes murder in the first degree a crime is not covered by civil law. This crime, then, would not be tried in a civil court.

19. **(2)** is the correct answer. Paragraph five says that laws that are unconstitutional cannot be enforced. Therefore, people cannot be punished for breaking them.

20. **(5)** is the correct answer. All the other choices deal only with certain kinds of laws or parts of the way they work. Only (5) expresses the purpose of all laws.

21. **(4)** is the correct answer. (1) and (2) are too general. (3) is not mentioned. (5) is too specific because many rights were discussed.

22. **(2)** is the correct answer. See the fifth paragraph. A person may, however, be retried on a different charge (4).

23. **(4)** is the correct answer. It is the only choice that is false. Trial by jury is guaranteed by the Sixth Amendment.

24. **(3)** is the correct answer. (1) and (4) would not happen. (2) and (5) could happen whether a person were told his or her rights or not.

25. **(3)** is the correct answer. It can be found in the second paragraph and the last one.

26. **(3)** is the correct answer. (5) is briefly discussed. The main topic is how the president comes to office by means of the electoral system.

27. (**2**) is the correct answer. The vice-president is chosen by the Senate. (1), (4) and (5) are not true.

28. (**2**) is the correct answer. The writer says that states with large populations have the most influence. The number of electoral votes a state can cast is based on the number of representatives the state has. This number is based on the population of the state.

29. (**1**) is the correct answer. The people are asking if they can't find another way or route to elect presidents. None of the animals exists today. The cartoonist thinks the electoral process they represent should not exist today.

30. (**4**) is the correct answer. The author suggests this in several places, especially the last two paragraphs. (1) *may* have been true, but is not true now, in the author's view. (5) is not true. There is no way of knowing how the author feels about (2) or (3).

UNIT IV: HISTORY

History is everything that people have ever done and the story or record of those events.

Directions: **The next passages cover topics in history. Each one starts with a few Key Words. The Key Words will give you an idea of what the passage is about. They are used in the passage along with other words that might be new. You will be able to figure out the meanings of some new words as you read them in the passage. Look up all new words in the Glossary at the end of the book, or use a dictionary.**

There are five reading skill questions to answer after each passage. Make a check (✓) next to the BEST answer for each question. Be sure to read all five choices first. Check your work using the Answers and Explanations section at the end of the unit. It starts on page 115.

HISTORY PASSAGE 1

KEY WORDS

historian—(noun) a person who studies and interprets events and their causes
document—(noun) an official paper used as proof of something
source—(noun) a point of original information
interpretation—(noun) an explanation; the act of explaining something

Historians agree that all events have causes. In history, one event can cause another event to happen. An example in American history is the American Revolution. In the early 1700s, the American colonists were unhappy with the way

England was treating them. This unhappiness was one important cause of the Revolution.

Historians study papers, records and documents that tell them about events. Historians are like detectives looking for clues. When they find clues, they put them all together like the pieces of a puzzle. The results give them an explanation of why things happened the way they did. When they look at the completed puzzle they can also find clues about what might happen in the future.

The work of the historian falls into three parts. First, he or she must find sources for the event being studied. Historians find their clues in newspapers, letters, church and town records, books and government records. They might find clues that are not written down. Roads, buildings, paintings, pottery and furniture might give historians clues to past events.

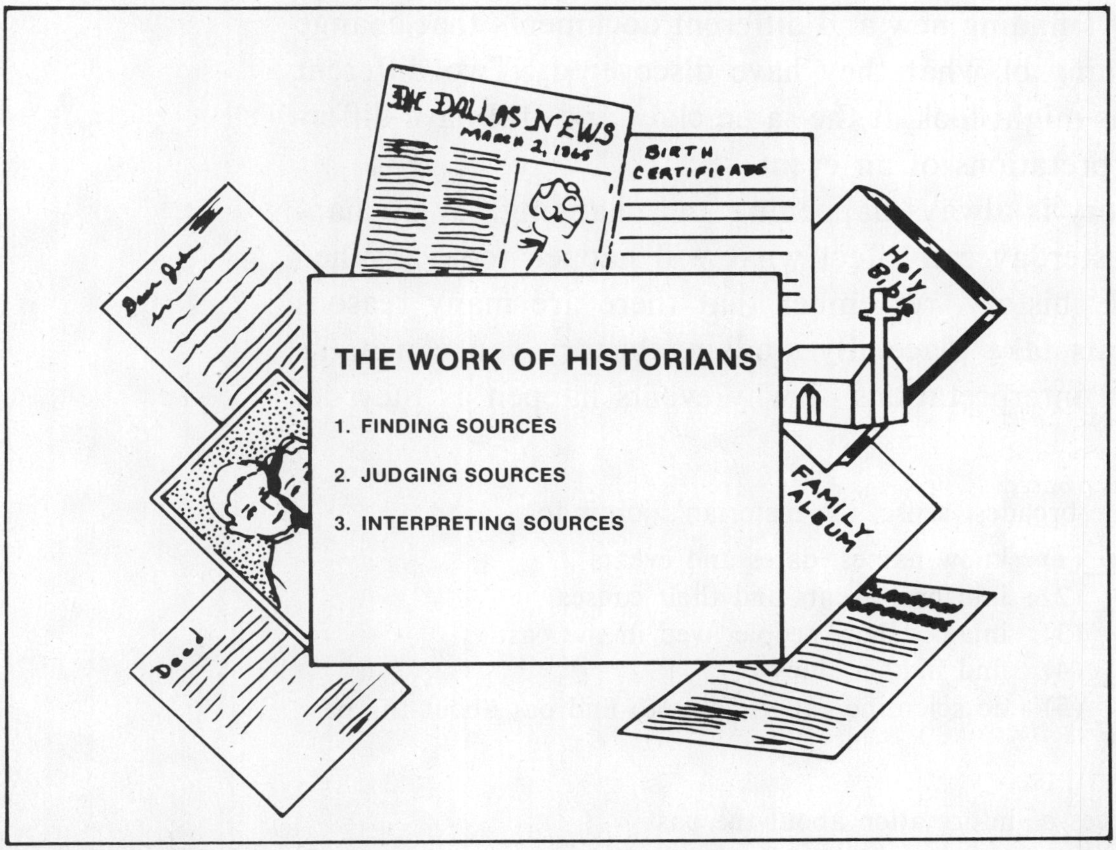

The second part of the historian's work is to decide whether the sources are good. Was the letter really written in 1862? Or was it written five years later? An old book might have been changed if it was printed again years after it was written. Does the old woman remember the right date her husband was killed? The historian must make sure this information is correct.

The final part of the historian's work is to draw together the many clues and make a whole picture. The historian must interpret the clues and decide what they mean. The historian must be good at finding sources and evaluating them. He or she must also be able to imagine the way people lived in the past. The historian must be able to see things through the eyes of the people being studied to better understand why they acted the way they did.

History is not a science like chemistry or physics. Any historian's <u>interpretation</u> will depend on which records are studied and how other events in history are seen. Historians are always finding new and different documents that change the meaning of what they have discovered. Two different historians might look at the same clues and still have different interpretations of an event.

History is always happening and changing. What happened yesterday can affect what will happen today. When you study history, remember that there are many reasons why events take place. By studying history you can make your own interpretations of why events happen as they do.

1. In the broadest sense, the historian's job is to

   ______(1) know names, dates and events
   ______(2) interpret events and their causes
   ______(3) imagine how people lived in the past
   ______(4) find hidden clues
   ______(5) do scientific experiments to find out about the past

2. Sources of information about the past

   ______(1) have all been studied

______(2) are always found in libraries
______(3) are usually accurate
______(4) must never be believed
______(5) must always be checked

3. If an important man says he was born in 1896, but his birth certificate says he was born in 1900, the historian should
______(1) believe the man
______(2) believe the birth certificate
______(3) find out why the man is lying
______(4) find out why the dates might be different
______(5) report the man to the police

4. Every event
______(1) can be predicted
______(2) has a history
______(3) will happen again
______(4) has been studied
______(5) has totally different causes

5. Historians' interpretations of the past
______(1) are all the same
______(2) never change
______(3) are not their main job
______(4) can change because of new events or information
______(5) are not affected by current events

Answers begin on page 115.

HISTORY PASSAGE 2

KEY WORDS

colony—(noun) a group of people who settle in a new place but keep ties to their homeland
colonist—(noun) a person living in a colony

In the early part of the 16th century, Spain was the most powerful country in the world. Spain owned Mexico and

Peru and was getting rich from the gold and silver that was mined there. England, seeking to increase her own influence as a world power, also wanted more gold and silver. So, James, the king of England, sent a trading company to the New World to find the same kinds of wealth the Spanish had found.

This English trading company founded the colony of Jamestown in Virginia in 1607. They soon realized that they were not going to get rich quickly. Instead of gold and silver they found swamps, forests and Indians. The early years were very hard ones. Though many people died aboard ship on the way over, many more died in Jamestown. The weather was harsh and the settlers lived on the food they brought with them. When this food ran out, they fought with each other and the Indians for survival.

By 1609 the colony began to grow. Houses and churches were being built and 30 acres of land had been planted. The population of Jamestown had grown to 500. But this growth brought trouble too. The Indians were angered as the settlers took over more of what had been Indian lands. The colonists built a fort to protect themselves from hostile Indians.

Two years had passed and life in Jamestown was still hard. Some settlers decided that it was too tough and they went back to England. After the winter of 1609-1610, new settlers came to the colony. But when they arrived, they found only 65 people left. So many people had died it came to be called "The Starving Time."

Captain John Smith named himself the leader of the survivors. He had been one of the first leaders when the settlers arrived in 1607. But the other leaders had disliked him and would not listen to him. Now they had no choice. The settlers were starving and fighting with the Indians and didn't know how to survive. Smith forced everyone to work and threatened to kick out anyone who wouldn't. He showed them how to build better houses, farm the land and live in peace with the Indians.

As more people came to Jamestown, the colony began to grow. Settlers saw that tobacco grew well in Virginia and started plantations to raise it. There weren't enough people to work these large farms. White workers, called indentured servants, were brought in from Europe. Black people from African countries were brought in and forced into slavery. As plantations spread south to the warmer climate and better soil, slavery spread with it.

PRODUCTS AND SETTLERS OF EARLY 17th CENTURY AMERICA

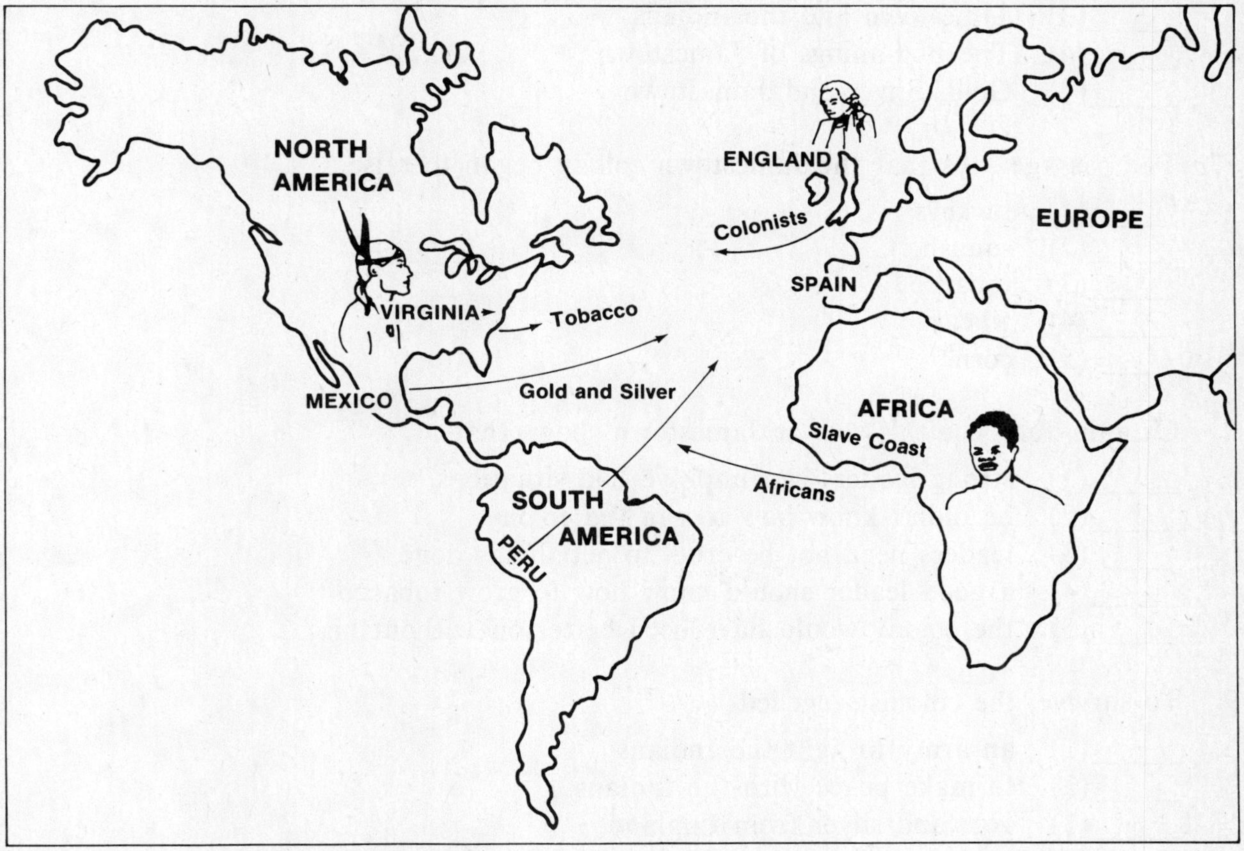

After ten years in the New World, no one in Jamestown had gotten rich from silver or gold. Instead, a new society was unfolding. People built their own houses, churches, schools and plantations. Because England was so far away, they began to govern themselves. They elected their own governor and wrote their own laws. People from each part of Jamestown and each plantation took part in the new government. They called themselves the House of Burgesses. This was the first self-governing group of colonists in America, but it was only open to free white people. The seeds of self-government and future racial problems had been planted in the New World.

6. The best title for this passage is
______(1) Captain John Smith
______(2) Starvation in Jamestown
______(3) Jamestown and the Indians
______(4) The Beginnings of Jamestown
______(5) Gold, Silver and Jamestown

7. The passage says that the Jamestown colony began to raise
______(1) turkeys
______(2) squash
______(3) tobacco
______(4) wheat
______(5) corn

8. Captain John Smith's role at Jamestown shows that
______(1) strong leaders can improve bad situations
______(2) he didn't know how to run the colony
______(3) leaders need not be cruel to get things done
______(4) a good leader should know how to grow tobacco
______(5) the colony would have been better off without him

9. To survive, the colonists needed
______(1) an army to fight the Indians
______(2) to make peace with the Indians
______(3) gold and silver from England
______(4) food from King James to trade with the Indians
______(5) to get rid of the House of Burgesses

10. The way Jamestown ended up governing itself probably
______(1) did not help the colony grow
______(2) helped the Indians
______(3) paved the way for American independence from England
______(4) was useless because many people moved south
______(5) was like the government of Spain

Answers begin on page 115.

HISTORY PASSAGE 3

KEY WORDS

Reconstruction—(noun) the period in American history (1865-1876) when freedmen and others tried to rebuild the war-torn South after the Civil War

freedman—(noun) a black person freed from slavery after the Civil War

Americans fought each other in the Civil War from 1861-1865. The end of the war brought about many changes in the South. Many of the farms, factories and businesses in the South had been destroyed. More than four million black people were set free from years of bondage. The South had to face the problems of rebuilding its cities and towns and of accepting black people as full and equal members of its society.

The period after the war was called Reconstruction. It was a time for rebuilding the South so that it could become part of the nation again. Blacks, called freedmen after the war, still worked for whites, often on the same land where they had been slaves. Instead of being paid in cash for their work, they were allowed to keep part of the crops they raised. This was called sharecropping. Poor whites who had lost everything in the war also became sharecroppers.

During Reconstruction, blacks were granted the right to vote. They could now hold political offices. They could build their own houses and schools. In 1866 the Fourteenth Amendment to the Constitution of the United States gave black people equal rights under the law. In 1870 the Fifteenth Amendment was passed. It said that no one could be denied the right to vote because of skin color or because he or she had been a slave.

Because of the Fourteenth and Fifteenth Amendments, no one could legally take away the rights of black people. But secret terrorist groups, such as the Ku Klux Klan (K.K.K.), threatened many black families. These groups used violence and fear to take away the rights black people had just fought for.

Because of this, northern soldiers stayed in the South for ten years after the Civil War to protect black people. But in 1876 everything changed. That year, there was a very close presidential election between the Republicans (Northerners) and the Democrats (Southerners). The southern whites in the Democratic Party said they would vote for the Republican candidate, Rutherford B. Hayes, if the northern troops would leave the South. The Republicans agreed and Hayes was elected president.

With the troops gone, the South tried to get back on its feet. But for black people this meant trouble. They began to lose all of the rights they had gained during Reconstruction after the war. They were threatened by the K.K.K. and treated badly by other white people. Many whites acted as if blacks were second-class citizens. Blacks were segregated, or kept separate from whites. Blacks could not get the same kinds of housing, schools or jobs that white people could. Not until the 1950s did the federal government begin to face some of the problems that slavery had created and that Reconstruction had not solved.

11. During a brief period after the Civil War, the federal government tried to

_____(1) wipe out sharecropping
_____(2) punish the South and keep it from rebuilding
_____(3) protect the rights of states to make their own laws about slavery
_____(4) rebuild the economy of the South and carry out the Constitutional amendments regarding equal rights
_____(5) keep blacks from voting

12. Federal troops left the South ten years after Reconstruction began because

_____(1) the Republicans and Democrats made a deal in order to elect President Hayes
_____(2) the Ku Klux Klan forced them out
_____(3) their work was done and the South had been rebuilt
_____(4) the Fourteenth and Fifteenth Amendments could now protect the rights of blacks
_____(5) sharecropping had become a way of life for many people

13. The struggle of American blacks for the rights granted them in the Constitution
    ______(1) was over after the Civil War
    ______(2) has never been aided by the federal government
    ______(3) was supported by groups such as the Ku Klux Klan
    ______(4) has roots in Reconstruction
    ______(5) has been without violence from either side

14. The history of Reconstruction shows that
    ______(1) the federal government can do whatever it sets out to do
    ______(2) federal laws are always obeyed
    ______(3) the South was wrong
    ______(4) the problems of ending slavery were easily solved
    ______(5) laws that protect peoples' rights will not always be obeyed

15. You can conclude that during Reconstruction
    ______(1) violence and discrimination against blacks stopped
    ______(2) the South was ready to change its ways
    ______(3) the problems of former slaves were not solved
    ______(4) blacks quickly became full and equal members of society
    ______(5) no one could disobey the Fourteenth and Fifteenth Amendments

Answers begin on page 115.

HISTORY PASSAGE 4

KEY WORDS

industrialization—(noun) the growth of businesses and factories

immigrant—(noun) a person who leaves his or her home to settle in a new country

After the Civil War, many people began to move westward. People in the South had lost their homes, businesses and jobs. They were looking for new places to settle. They were ready to start over. Businesses in the North were growing. They needed more room and new markets for their goods.

To encourage people to move west, the federal government passed the Homestead Act in 1862. This new law gave free land to farmers. Anyone could get 160 acres of land by agreeing to live on it and grow a crop within five years. Other laws gave a lot of land to the railroads and other big businesses.

Many people were moving west. But they needed the goods and products made in eastern factories. The railroads filled the gap. They moved a lot of manufactured goods to all parts of the country. This was the age of industrialization.

At first, the farmers along the railroad lines got along well with the railroad owners. The railroads brought machinery to the farmers and took the farmers' crops back to the cities. But in the end, the railroads began charging more and more for their services. The farmers thought they were being cheated and formed a group called the Grange to fight for their rights. The farmers elected their own people to government. These people passed many laws to help the small farmer, including laws that defined what the railroad owners could and could not do.

The first railroad to reach across the country to California was the Transcontinental Railroad. It was built mainly by Irish and Chinese immigrants. These were people who had left their homes in Ireland and China to come to America. The railroads also brought other immigrants to the new cities and towns that grew up along the railroad routes.

Sometimes the railroads treated people who worked for them unfairly. They lowered workers' wages and demanded longer hours from them. Like the farmers who started the Grange, the workers formed unions to protect themselves. The unions argued with the railroad owners about wages, working conditions, work schedules and insurance. When the union and the railroad bosses disagreed, the workers went on strike. They refused to work until both groups agreed.

By the 1890s railroads had made industrialization possible throughout the country. People and goods could go from coast to coast faster than ever before. Cities and towns grew up, and areas of the West that had been territories became states.

THE U.S. RAILROAD SYSTEM—1860

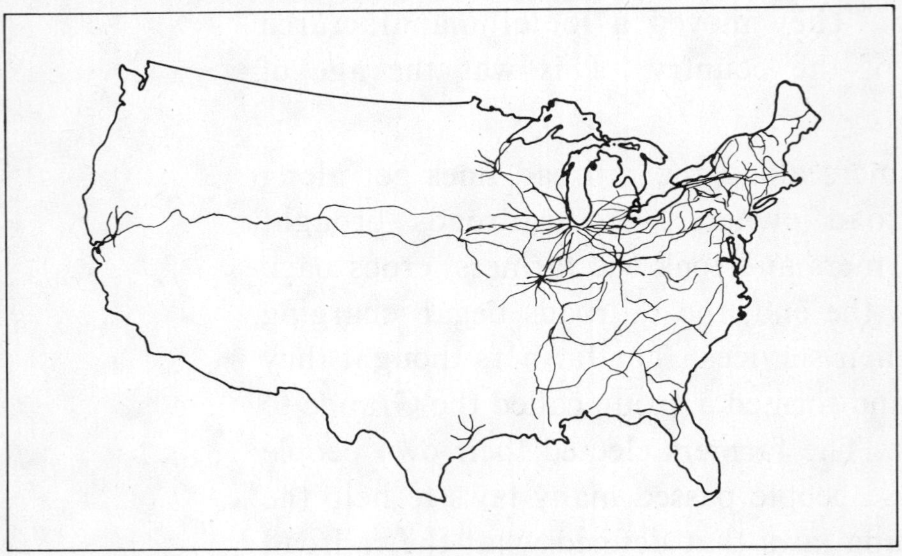

THE U.S. RAILROAD SYSTEM—1900

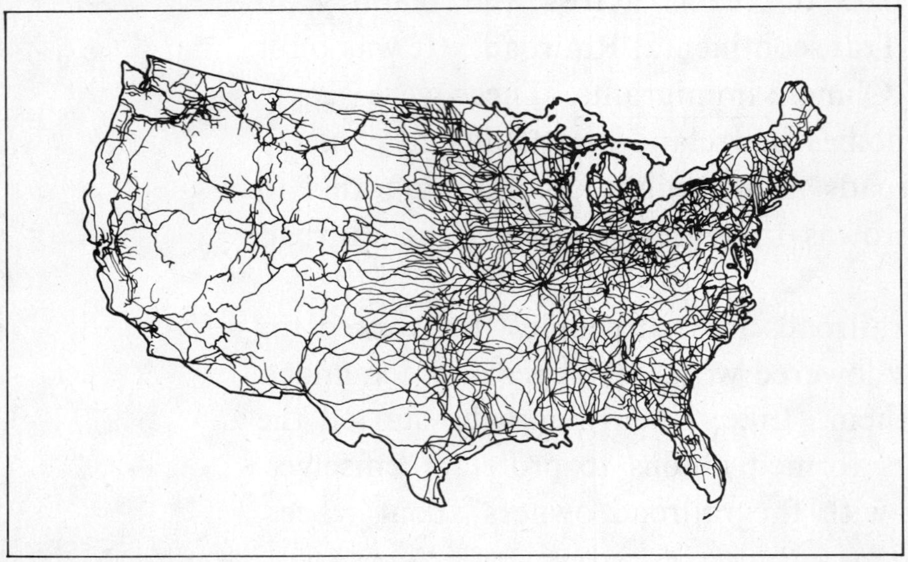

16. The main idea of this passage is that
______(1) immigrants from several countries built the railroads
______(2) farmers had to fight the railroad interests by forming the Grange
______(3) the U.S. expanded westward after the Civil War
______(4) the Homestead Act gave farmers 160 acres of free land
______(5) the Transcontinental Railroad was built to help move people west

17. Many of the people who built the railroads were
______(1) Puerto Rican and Mexican immigrants
______(2) immigrants from China and Ireland
______(3) slaves and free men
______(4) American Indians
______(5) cowboys and farmers

18. The passage shows that in order to develop nationwide industry, any large country would need
______(1) to keep people from forming unions
______(2) to develop its own machines
______(3) people from other countries to do the work
______(4) a national system of transportation like railroads
______(5) farm organizations like the Grange

19. The railroads not only moved machines, products and people, but also
______(1) made many towns and cities grow
______(2) made many states become territories
______(3) charged immigrants to come to the U.S. and work
______(4) supported organizations like the Grange
______(5) moved the houses of people in the South after the Civil War

20. From this passage it is clear that farmers and workers
______(1) had no power over what the railroads did
______(2) did not want immigrants to come and build the railroads
______(3) fought with each other to control the railroads
______(4) did not take land under the Homestead Act
______(5) played a big part in making laws to control railroads

Answers begin on page 116.

HISTORY PASSAGE 5

KEY WORDS

territory—(noun) land which is under the control of a distant government but which does not have the full rights of a state or province

imperialism—(noun) spreading the power and wealth of a nation by taking over other lands

By the 1890s, industrialization in the United States had spread from coast to coast. Businesses and factories were making so many goods and products that there weren't enough people to buy them all. A recession in 1890-1891 caused many people to lose their jobs. During the depression of 1893 there was little money and even fewer jobs.

Other industrial countries like England and Germany had the same problems. But they solved their problems by taking over lands in other parts of the world. This meant that they sent their people to settle the new territories in the same way that Europeans had started colonies in America. Often this meant using force to take over these lands. Getting land and power this way is called imperialism.

By taking over distant lands, the European countries gained new markets for their goods. The new territories also gave them cheap raw materials needed to make these goods.

Many of the countries they took over were not Christian and did not have any white people. Most white, Christian Europeans in power felt superior to all non-whites. They said these people were backward and unable to take care of themselves. Of course this kind of idea is racist and untrue. But the powerful whites used it as an excuse to take over other countries.

At about this time, the United States was also becoming imperialistic. The government and big businesses in the U.S.

were interested in some small island countries in the Pacific Ocean. They also had their eye on two countries that are very close to the U.S.—Cuba and Puerto Rico. Both of these countries were owned by Spain, but Cubans and Puerto Ricans were fighting the Spanish to be free. There had been many revolutions in Cuba and Puerto Rico and in the far away Philippine Islands in the Pacific Ocean.

American newspapers carried many stories about Spanish cruelty in these island countries. The people behind the newspapers and perhaps the government and big business wanted Americans to become angry enough to go to war with Spain. At the same time, America was building factories in these countries. American businesses wanted the same kinds of economic advantages that the European countries were getting by taking over other lands. American newspapers called the people of those countries "little brown brothers." Stories about the suffering of the people turned Americans against Spain.

WHERE THE FIGHTING TOOK PLACE

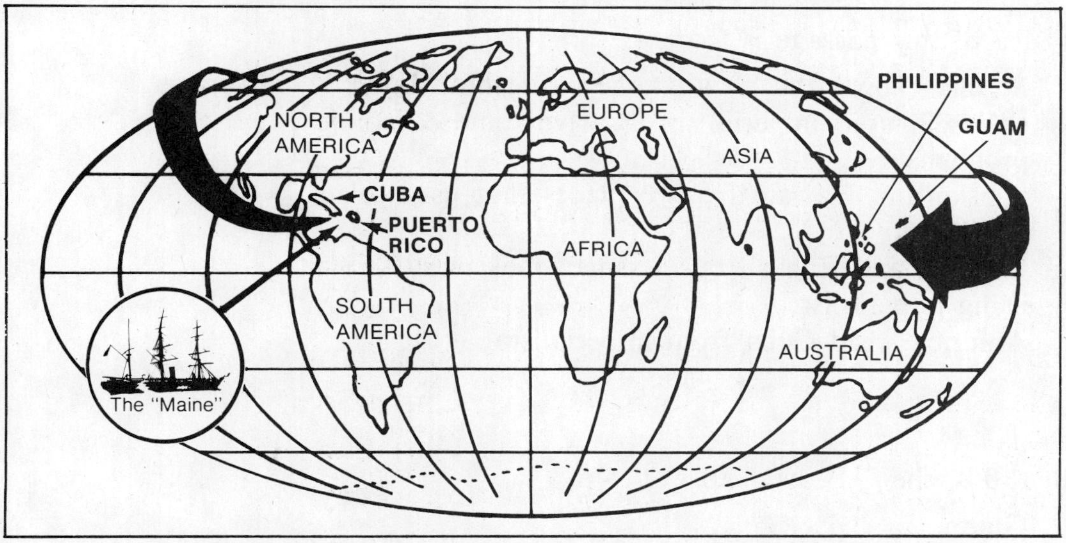

After the "Maine" blew up in Cuban waters, fighting broke out on both sides of the globe. The end of the Spanish-American War brought Cuba, Puerto Rico, the Philippines and Guam under direct U.S. control.

In 1898 the American battleship Maine was blown up while docked in Cuba. The U.S. blamed Spain and declared war. But the war didn't last very long because Spain was no match for the U.S. As a result of losing the war, Spain was forced to give its territories to the United States.

This meant that the United States took over Cuba and Puerto Rico in the Atlantic Ocean and the Philippines and Guam in the Pacific Ocean. The U.S. kept many troops in the Philippines because it said that the people there needed American protection. The U.S. also said that it wanted to protect all of these countries from other imperialists. At about the same time, the U.S. took over the Hawaiian Islands.

In the early 1900s, Cuba became an independent nation, free of U.S. control. Later, so did the Philippines and Guam. Other U.S. territories like Hawaii and Alaska have since become states. Puerto Rico is still a U.S. territory, although some people there want independence. The U.S., once a colony, became a world power with territories of its own.

21. The main idea of this passage is that

_____(1) no one knows who blew up the battleship Maine
_____(2) the U.S. used imperialism to solve some economic problems
_____(3) Alaska and Hawaii are two places that used to be territories
_____(4) German and English businessmen took over Africa using imperialism
_____(5) America freed Cuba from imperialism

22. In the late 1800s, the U.S. went to war with

_____(1) Guam
_____(2) Hawaii
_____(3) Cuba
_____(4) Spain
_____(5) England

23. From the information given, it is clear that
______(1) business interests can have a big effect on a government's actions
______(2) the U.S. and Spain will be enemies for a long time
______(3) imperialism is good for small countries
______(4) Christians are better than other people
______(5) Puerto Rico is not ready to be independent

24. What the passage says about Puerto Rico suggests that
______(1) the people there are very poor
______(2) some people there do not want to be a U.S. territory
______(3) the people there were better off under Spanish rule
______(4) Americans love freedom more than Cubans
______(5) businessmen think Puerto Rico should be independent

25. You can conclude that U.S. imperialism helped
______(1) relations with England and Germany
______(2) U.S. business interests
______(3) prevent a worldwide war
______(4) the Spanish government
______(5) Puerto Rico gain independence

Answers begin on page 116.

HISTORY PASSAGE 6

KEY WORDS

depression—(noun) in economic terms, a time when business is very slow, production is cut back and many people are out of work

ally—(noun) a friend; a country that joins with another country to achieve some goal

World War II was the second great war fought in the 20th century. It lasted from 1939 to 1945. Fighting took place all over the world. Nearly 40 million people were killed. Nearly 65 nations took part.

There are many reasons why World War II happened, but historians agree that there were two main reasons. One reason is that World War I, which began in 1914, never really ended. During the first part of the century, Germany began taking over other European countries by force. It also took over land around the world. When Germany lost World War I, it lost all of its territories. The United States, England and France cut the size of the German army so it could not start a war again.

It was just a matter of time before Germany would try to regain its power. In the 1930s, Adolf Hitler began promising the German people that he would make Germany great again. Hitler was the head of a German political party called the Nazi Party. He soon became the leader of all of Germany. Hitler said that the German people were the greatest race of people on Earth and that other countries were taking advantage of Germany by trying to keep it weak.

In the 1930s, the leaders of Japan and Italy followed Hitler's lead. They, too, felt that they were being kept weak by the other powers of the world.

Historians say that economic causes were the second reason for World War II. The U.S., England and France wanted the losers of World War I to pay for everything that had been damaged. The Western countries wanted this money to rebuild their economies. The United States also wanted all money returned that had been loaned to other countries to fight the war. These were some of the reasons for the Great Depression.

The Great Depression happened in the 1930s. It was a time of little money and few jobs. By this time, Germany, Japan and Italy were allies. They called themselves the Axis Powers. The Axis Powers told their people that the Depression was caused by the Western countries. Hitler also made Jewish people the scapegoat for Germany's economic problems. He had millions of Jews and other people the Nazis didn't like arrested or killed.

Countries all over the world were affected by what came to be called the Great Depression. For those who thought the second world war began for economic reasons, it was said that the Axis Powers started World War II to avoid paying back the money they owed. Going to war meant their economies would improve. When the war started, the Great Depression ended. It is hoped that going to war does not become an answer to today's economic problems.

26. The main idea of this passage is that

_____(1) the Great Depression ruined Germany's economy
_____(2) historians think World War II started for two important economic and political reasons
_____(3) 40 million people were killed during World War II
_____(4) Germany and Japan were allies during World War II
_____(5) Germany, Italy and Japan started World War II

27. The United States, England and France

_____(1) were the Axis Powers
_____(2) promised to make Germany great again

_____(3) ended the Great Depression
_____(4) reduced the size of Germany's army after World War I
_____(5) did not fight in World War I

28. The causes of World War II led to the idea that bad economic conditions in the world today
_____(1) could not start a war
_____(2) should be blamed on the Nazi Party
_____(3) could start wars as they've done in the past
_____(4) should be blamed on Germany
_____(5) are not the concern of the United States

29. After World War II started,
_____(1) the German economy probably improved for a while
_____(2) the German people were the greatest race of people on Earth
_____(3) the Great Depression started again
_____(4) money disappeared
_____(5) the American economy got worse

30. From this passage, we can conclude that
_____(1) there will probably never be another world war
_____(2) the causes of wars between countries are often economic and political
_____(3) trouble starts when countries begin to band together
_____(4) no country's army should be bigger than that of another country
_____(5) Hitler was the true cause of World War II

Answers begin on page 116.

ANSWERS AND EXPLANATIONS—HISTORY

1. **(2)** is the best answer. (1), (3) and (4) are all part of what historians do. (5) is not true. History is not a science like chemistry or physics.

2. **(5)** is the correct answer. The other answers are not true. The passage says that historians must act like detectives to check their clues and information.

3. **(4)** is the correct answer. Historians should look for reasons. They must not jump to conclusions. The man may be right, or he might have changed his age at some time in his life for some reason. An error could also have been made on his birth certificate.

4. **(2)** is the correct answer. The causes of even small events can be found in the events and circumstances that came before. This is what makes up history.

5. **(4)** is the correct answer. New interpretations of the same events are always being made because of changing information or new ways of looking at what happened.

6. **(4)** is correct. All the other choices are only details which are part of the story of the beginnings of Jamestown.

7. **(3)** is correct. Find this detail in paragraph six.

8. **(1)** is correct. The settlers, according to paragraph five, were starving and fighting, and they didn't know how to survive. Captain John Smith did things as a leader which solved these problems. Therefore, it seems that strong leaders can improve bad situations.

9. **(2)** is correct. Since paragraph five says that fighting with the Indians was one problem the settlers had that was keeping them from surviving, it is clear that they needed to make peace with the Indians.

10. **(3)** is correct. The last paragraph says that the people of Jamestown formed the first self-governing group in America, far away from England. Self-government was an important first step toward American independence from England.

11. **(4)** is the correct answer. These were the goals of Reconstruction.

12. **(1)** is the correct answer. This detail can be found in the fifth paragraph.

13. **(4)** is the correct answer. The other answers are not true.

14. **(5)** is the correct answer. (3) is not an idea that can be inferred from the passage. (1), (2) and (4) cannot be inferred from this passage either.

15. **(3)** is the correct answer. The war was over, but the problems of former slaves were still present.

16. **(3)** is the correct answer. All the other choices are details about the passage, not the main idea.

17. **(2)** is the correct answer. Check it with paragraph five.

18. **(4)** is the correct answer. Paragraph one says that growing businesses needed new markets for their goods. Paragraph three tells how railroads moved goods to all parts of the country. So it follows that industry must be able to move its products from place to place to sell them. Therefore, a big country needs a national transportation system.

19. **(1)** is the correct answer. Paragraph five says that railroads brought immigrants to towns and cities along their routes. Paragraph seven says that the U.S. was united by railroads and that cities and towns grew up in the West. Therefore, you can guess that the railroads made many towns and cities grow.

20. **(5)** is the correct answer. Paragraphs four and six give information about how farmers and workers influenced railroad laws by forming unions and organizations like the Grange.

21. **(2)** is the correct answer. (5) is false and all the other answers are just details about the main idea.

22. **(4)** is correct. Paragraph seven gives you this fact. The U.S. fought the war in Cuba, but it was a war against Spain.

23. **(1)** is correct. Imperialism got new markets for U.S. goods and cheap raw materials to make those goods. Imperialism was something businesses used. Businessmen got the U.S. govern-

ment to take control of other countries. Therefore, this passage gives you the idea that business interests can have a big effect on a government's actions.

24. **(2)** is correct. The last paragraph states that some people in Puerto Rico want independence. Those who feel this way do not want to be a U.S. territory.

25. **(2)** is correct. Since the main idea of the passage is that the U.S. used imperialism to solve economic problems, we can conclude that imperialism helped U.S. business interests.

26. **(2)** is the correct answer. All the other choices are details, but not the main idea. The main idea is stated in paragraph two.

27. **(4)** is the correct answer. This detail is in the second paragraph. All the other choices are not true.

28. **(3)** is the correct answer. Bad economic conditions contributed to the start of World War II, and they could contribute to the start of wars today. The other answers are false and do not apply the ideas covered in the passage about how World War II started.

29. **(1)** is the correct answer. Paragraph six explains that going to war meant their economies would improve. Since World War II caused the Great Depression to end, Germany's economy probably improved for a while.

30. **(2)** is the correct answer. We can come to this conclusion based on the whole passage.

UNIT V: BEHAVIORAL SCIENCE

Behavioral science is the study of how and why people act, think and feel as they do. It looks at individuals and social groups.

Directions: **The next passages cover topics from behavioral science. Each one starts with Key Words. The Key Words will give you an idea of what the passage is about. They are used in the passage along with other words that might be new. You will be able to figure out the meanings of some new words from the way they are used in the passage. Look up all new words in the Glossary at the end of the book or use a dictionary.**

After each passage, there are five reading skill questions to answer. Check (✓) the BEST answer for each question. Use the Answers and Explanations to check your work. They are at the end of the unit starting on page 138.

BEHAVIORAL SCIENCE PASSAGE 1

KEY WORDS

individual—(noun) a single human being; one person (adjective) one; separate; having to do with a single person or thing

society—(noun) a lasting group of people that usually live together in a certain area, and see themselves as sharing a culture; a set system of roles for people and ideas about expected behavior; systems or institutions to meet all basic human needs

culture—(noun) the way of life of a society; the society's knowledge, beliefs, art, morals, laws and customs

The individual, society and culture—these words sum up three ways scientists study people and human behavior.

Psychology, sociology and anthropology are the major fields of study in behavioral science. (Sometimes even history, political science and economics are thought of as fields of behavioral science.)

THE THREE MAIN BRANCHES OF BEHAVIORAL SCIENCE

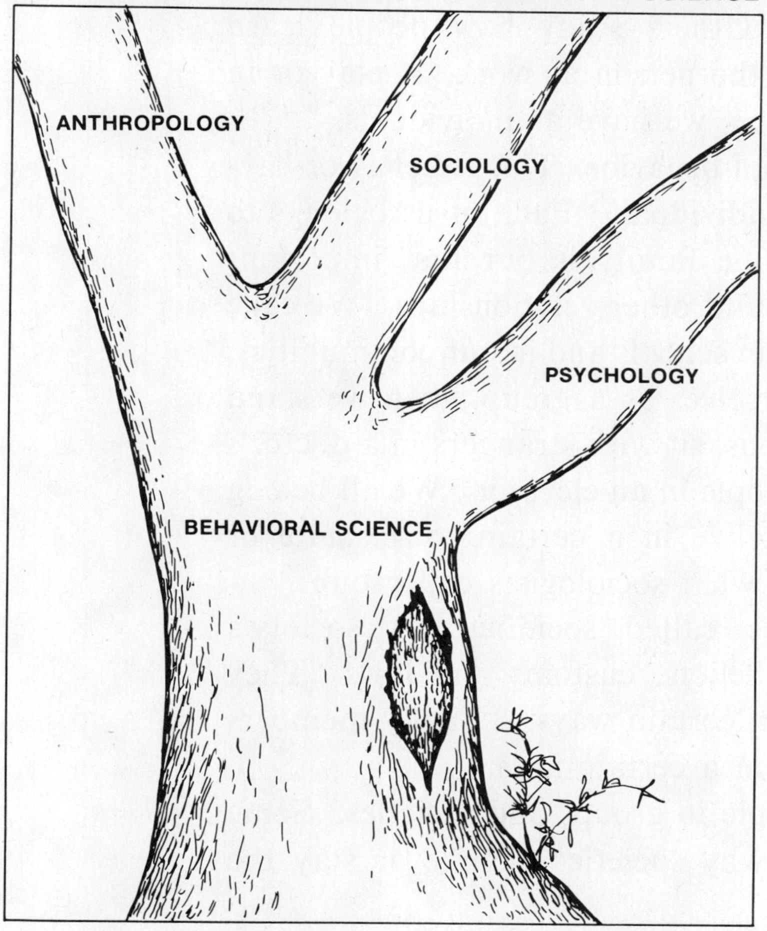

Psychology is the study of the individual person. Sociology, on the other hand, is the study of societies and groups of people. Anthropology, to go a step further, is the study of culture. In each of these fields there are lots of topics or areas to study. In each of these fields the topics can be studied in many different ways. In each of these fields many behavioral scientists have worked to build ideas and use those ideas to better understand human beings. This unit will focus on some of the topics studied by behavioral scientists. It will look at some well-known ideas that have added to what we know about behavior. First, let's take a closer look at the three fields.

Psychology is seen both as the study of individual behavior and as the study of how the mind works. It is the study of people and other animals. Some psychologists look at how a person grows and ages. Others study how people learn things. Still others study the person at work, at play or in any of the other experiences we have as individuals.

Sociology looks at social behavior. This is behavior having to do with groups of individuals. Each of us belongs to many kinds of groups. The family is our first important group. As we grow, we build other relationships. We take part in group life at work, in schools and in our communities. We can even think of ourselves as a group when we stand with others waiting for a bus, sit with strangers in a doctor's office or ride with other people in an elevator. We all belong to racial groups. We all live in a certain town, state or country. All of these are what sociologists call groups.

Some groups can be called societies. A society's members share a set of beliefs, customs and laws. They expect each other to act in certain ways. Usually members of a society live together in a certain area.

Sociologists study people in groups and societies. Some try to find out how and why societies change or stay the same.

Anthropology can cover how people of different cultures are alike and how they are different. It can look at cultures of today and cultures of the past. Some anthropologists look at physical differences between people of different cultures. Others study culture traits like smoking, eating with a fork, taking part in holidays, playing basketball or believing in spirits. Alone, the traits may have little meaning. When studied within the whole culture, the full meaning can sometimes be seen.

Psychology, sociology and anthropology, then, show us many ways to look at life. Some behavioral scientists are mainly interested in doing research. Their work helps to uncover new facts and ideas about behavior. Others are more interested in using what is known to help people learn, work, grow and live better.

1. The main idea of this passage is about
   _____(1) differences among sociologists
   _____(2) why history, political science and economics are fields of behavioral science
   _____(3) the three major fields of behavioral science
   _____(4) why people of different cultures are different
   _____(5) how psychologists study the mind of the individual

2. The study of how people act in groups is called
   _____(1) anthropology
   _____(2) culture
   _____(3) physics
   _____(4) sociology
   _____(5) psychology

3. You might learn about Eskimo religions in
   _____(1) an anthropology book
   _____(2) a physics text
   _____(3) a sociology passage
   _____(4) a psychology book
   _____(5) an economics text

4. According to this passage, the study of human behavior
   _____(1) is not the concern of sociologists or anthropologists
   _____(2) can be approached by looking at groups as well as at individuals
   _____(3) can best be done in a psychology laboratory
   _____(4) is more important to people than the study of physics
   _____(5) is an attempt to control the future of the world

5. Behavioral science
   _____(1) is a narrow, specific field
   _____(2) can never be of practical use to people
   _____(3) seeks insight into how the earth was formed
   _____(4) can predict the future
   _____(5) seeks insight into how people think, feel and act

Answers begin on page 138.

BEHAVIORAL SCIENCE PASSAGE 2

KEY WORDS

institution—(noun) a system of social roles and customs that serves an important need of a society
marriage—(noun) a basic social institution that sets the way for two people to come together and build a family unit
custom—(noun) a practice shared by a group of people

The raising of children is a basic need of all societies. Every society has some way to bring men and women together into families that will raise children. Most societies have set up an institution to handle this. In our society we call this institution marriage.

A man and a woman who get married can have children with the blessing of the society they live in. Their home, then, becomes a place where children are raised and cared for. In all societies families help teach children how to act. Families prepare children to live in the society. In this way every society gets a flow of new members.

Today in the U.S. most people think of marriage as a set of promises two people make to each other. They promise that they will love and care for each other. They promise they will live together for the rest of their lives. There are legal promises made in marriage, too. If a married person dies, the surviving member will get any money that person had. If the husband or wife leaves for some reason, the law says that he or she must help support the children, if there are any.

Not all cultures look at marriage the same way. In some cultures women have little to say about the person they marry. Marriages are set or arranged by parents. Sometimes this is done when the woman is still a child or even before she is born. This custom was once common all over the world. Marriage was seen as the joining of families. Parents would try to marry their daughters to men with money and power or to men from important families. In China and Japan marriages were often arranged by a marriage broker. This was a person whose job was to match people in marriage.

Another custom of marriage that may seem strange to us is called the bride's price. A man had to pay for a wife. The money went to the bride's family. This was a marriage custom in the Middle East, China and in some African countries. In European countries until the 1800s, it was a custom for a bride to bring her new husband a dowry. A dowry was money and gifts from the father of the bride.

Although the most basic purpose marriage serves is to have a way to raise families, marriage can mean many things. It can be the way two families join, the way money is passed on, how power is increased and how children are raised. Even today in some cultures, marriage is the means by which control of a woman is passed from her parents to her husband. The idea that people marry only because they love each other is fairly new.

Whatever the meaning of marriage, most societies see it as an important institution. Its customs and meanings tell us about the society and culture in which it exists.

6. The main point of this passage is that

______(1) marriage has no meaning without love

______(2) many cultures have no form of marriage

______(3) the institution of marriage is important to most societies

______(4) some cultures don't let the woman choose her husband

______(5) marriage can bring a family more power

7. In some cultures, marriage can mean passing control of a woman from her

_____(1) mother to her sister
_____(2) mother to her brother
_____(3) sister to her father
_____(4) parents to her husband
_____(5) mother to her father

8. In modern U.S. culture, the bride's parents usually pay for the wedding. In some ways, this is similar to the old custom of

_____(1) the bride's price
_____(2) the dowry
_____(3) the marriage broker
_____(4) love
_____(5) the arranged marriage

9. In the Middle East, China and parts of Africa, where paying a bride's price was a custom,

_____(1) a poor man might not be able to marry
_____(2) a rich man could have only one wife
_____(3) a poor man usually had many children
_____(4) a poor woman could marry only once
_____(5) a poor woman could only marry a rich man

10. The writer of this passage concludes that

_____(1) the old ways of marriage were cruel compared to the new ones
_____(2) women should not have gone along with some of the marriage customs of old cultures
_____(3) the people of Japan had better marriage customs than Americans
_____(4) there is no need for an institution called marriage
_____(5) marriage customs tell us something about how different cultures see the world

Answers begin on page 138.

BEHAVIORAL SCIENCE PASSAGE 3

KEY WORDS

conformity—(noun) following the rules; acting as your society or group expects you to

experiment—(noun) a test that is used to discover or prove something

subject—(noun) an individual who is studied in an experiment

Did you know that what your family and friends think can sometimes cause you to change what you think? When everyone around you disagrees with you, it may cause you to change your mind. You may feel that being accepted by people you care about is more important than your true opinions. You may also feel that if everyone else disagrees with you, they must be right.

Conformity means acting the same way as the people around you. It can also mean that you follow the rules of behavior that you think are expected of you. It can even mean that you feel you must or should think like the people around you.

An experiment was done to show how people conform. Seven people were placed in a room together. The person doing the experiment showed them two cards. On one card was a single line. On the other card were three lines. Each was a different length, but one of them was the same length as the line on the first card. (See the picture.)

Six of the people in the room had been told beforehand to pick the same wrong line. This meant that they would all

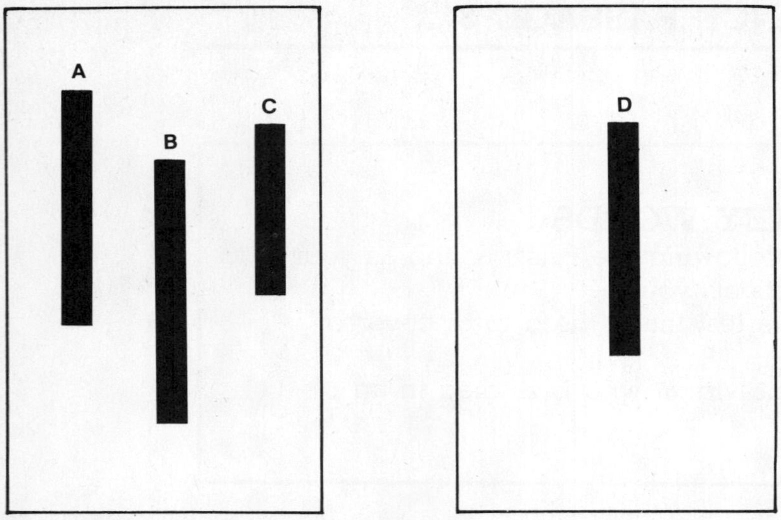

Six out of seven people in a psychology experiment said that line B was the same length as line D. Would you have agreed with them?

agree on a wrong answer on each pair of cards. The seventh person—the subject—would be confused when he or she heard one person after another give an answer that seemed wrong.

This experiment was tried 50 times. Each time, six people agreed to give the wrong answer, and a new person was the subject. About one-third of the people tested changed their answers and went along with what the six people said. This shows that we sometimes accept the opinion of the group even if we know it is wrong.

There are many kinds of conformity in the world around us. When people wear a certain style of clothes, it means that they are conforming to that style. When we try to be like our parents, we are conforming to our parents' values. These kinds of conformity can be helpful to us. They help us learn how to be accepted members of our community.

In other cases, as we have seen, conformity is not good. When people accept things they don't believe in or things they feel are wrong just because of what other people may say, we could have problems. It is not good for our society when people merely try to conform rather than think for themselves.

In behavioral science there have been experiments and studies of how conformity works. Scientists have looked at why people do or do not conform. They have also studied the good and bad sides of human conformity.

11. The main idea of this passage is that
 ______(1) conformity is wrong
 ______(2) people shouldn't try to influence other people's thinking
 ______(3) people often change their beliefs to conform with those of the larger group
 ______(4) conformity cannot be tested through experiments
 ______(5) everyone conforms most of the time

12. An experiment tested conformity by
 ______(1) asking a person to guess how other people answered
 ______(2) arranging with six of seven people to give a wrong answer
 ______(3) asking a question that had no right answer
 ______(4) testing people who all thought alike
 ______(5) asking a very difficult question

13. Based on the passage, you would think that voters in an election
 ______(1) could not be influenced by public opinion polls
 ______(2) would not need to know facts about the candidates
 ______(3) can be influenced by what others think about the candidates
 ______(4) should discuss the issues carefully
 ______(5) should not vote

14. Suppose a person is in a waiting room with four or five strangers. No one is smoking. The person wants to smoke. What is he or she likely to do, according to what this passage says about conformity?
 ______(1) ask the receptionist for an ashtray
 ______(2) quit smoking
 ______(3) light up and use the floor for an ashtray
 ______(4) ask people if they will mind the smoke
 ______(5) not smoke while in the waiting room

15. You could conclude that conformity
    ______(1) is usually correct and proper
    ______(2) is always a mindless copying of other people
    ______(3) should be encouraged more in our schools
    ______(4) should be discouraged in the family
    ______(5) should be seen as sometimes good and sometimes harmful

Answers begin on page 138.

BEHAVIORAL SCIENCE PASSAGE 4

KEY WORDS

social role—(noun) the rights, duties and expected behavior of a certain type of person in a social group or society

social change—(noun) something new in how a society or its institutions work; some change in family, religious or economic life, for example

Every society has systems of social roles that it teaches its members to play. The social role lays down the duties, rights and expected behavior for people. What is expected in any one social role is closely tied to other roles in the society. When there is a change in one, there will be wide changes in other parts of the society. Social change often starts with a small change in a social role. Expected behavior for men and women in a society (sex roles) are important social roles.

The social roles of women in the U.S. have begun to change. This, in turn, is affecting men's social roles, family life, how children are raised and many other parts of our daily lives.

In the past, women spent most of their time raising children and running their homes. Social roles for women centered mainly around family and home life. It was the woman's role to do everything needed to feed and clothe the family and keep the home comfortable. Most households were run by women. The social role for men was to support the family by working outside the home. The man was seen as the breadwinner.

Important changes are now being seen in our society. About half the women in the U.S. over age 16 have entered

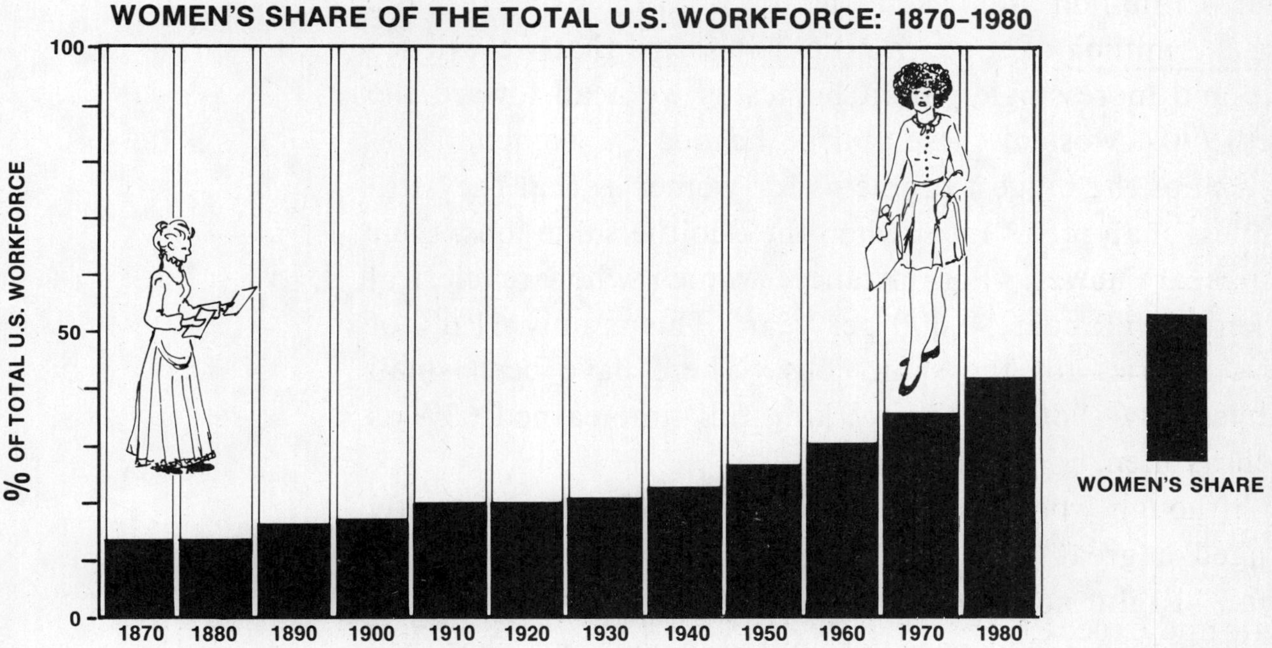

the paid work force. More than half the women with children work outside the home. The rising cost of living has forced many women to add to the family's income. For many, the two-paycheck family is a necessity. With more women working outside the home, some men are doing more to help raise the children, take care of the family and run the house. Finding other ways to raise children, such as in day care centers, is becoming more important. In addition, American families are shrinking. People are having fewer children. By 1990, 60 million American households will have no children under age 15. Women also are living longer than they did in the past. This means they are free to do other things with their lives. They can raise their children and then go back to work or back to school. These are some of the social changes we are now seeing.

Another change is in the number of families with only one parent. Some of these single-parent homes are headed by men raising children without women. The household headed by a woman is more common. In 1960 there were about 4.5 million families headed by women. By 1978 there were 8.2 million of these families. It seems that we will see more and more single-parent homes as we head toward the year 1990. Most of these will be headed by women.

One of the biggest problems for women is that they still earn less than men. Even when they do the same jobs, their salaries are lower. For instance, women who are clerical workers earn about $8,600 per year. This is only 61.6% of men's salaries for the same jobs. There have been small changes. By 1980 women working full time earned 63% as much as men.

Although women's and men's social roles have already changed a great deal, there may be more changes in the future. Right now there are almost as many women in college as men. People are not limited in choosing what they want to study or the kind of training they want. Greater numbers of jobs are being opened to women. People are becoming freer to choose the kind of work they want to do. At the same time, society is getting used to the idea of seeing women and men in new roles. We will see many other changes as our whole society shifts and grows.

16. The main idea of this passage is that
   ______(1) any woman who wants to can have a family as well as a full-time job
   ______(2) social roles of men and women have been the same for many years
   ______(3) women can never make as much money as men
   ______(4) families will not exist in the future if there is more social change
   ______(5) social roles of men and women are changing greatly

17. Between 1960 and 1978 families and households headed by women
   ______(1) stayed about the same in number
   ______(2) contained more young children
   ______(3) became much smaller in number
   ______(4) became much larger in number
   ______(5) were not counted

18. Based on the passage, we can guess that as social roles for black people keep changing, there will be
   ______(1) slow changes for other people outside the U.S.
   ______(2) changes only in U.S. employment
   ______(3) broader social changes for the whole society
   ______(4) no changes in the rest of society
   ______(5) small changes mainly for the people involved

19. Women working outside the home
   ______(1) cause prices to go up
   ______(2) are a cause and a result of social change
   ______(3) usually earn as much as men
   ______(4) have little effect on working men
   ______(5) are making families fall apart

20. The changes in the social roles of men and women
   ______(1) are easy to understand and accept
   ______(2) should not be allowed to happen
   ______(3) are harder on men than on women
   ______(4) affect only a small part of the population
   ______(5) have an effect on many areas of society

Answers begin on page 139.

BEHAVIORAL SCIENCE PASSAGE 5

KEY WORDS

elderly—(noun) an old person; the aged
(adjective) old; aged
gerontology—(noun) the study of aging and the problems of old people

Today there are more old people than ever before. In 1900, 4.1% of the people in the U.S. were age 65 or older. In 1981, 11% were age 65 or older. One of every nine Americans was at least 65 years old. By the year 2000, our elderly population will grow from 23 million to 32 million.

The field of gerontology is a behavioral science which studies the elderly and their needs. The whole process of how people age is of concern now as our population gets older. What is being learned now will change government and social programs that may one day affect us all. Gerontologists are correcting some of the myths about old age. At the same time they are uncovering new facts about aging. Their work has shown that the most common problems for older people are poor health, little money and loneliness.

Older people become sick much more often than younger people. Most of them are not as strong as they once were. This makes it harder for them to get well once they get sick. Many older people cannot see or hear as well as they once could. Often they cannot move as quickly as younger people.

Another major problem in old age is the loss of income that many old people experience. Today, most people stop working when they are 65 or 70 years old. In 1900 a person could work until he or she decided to retire. Now, many companies force people to stop working when they reach a certain age. They must retire even if they are still able and willing to do the job. The Social Security program helps many make ends meet once they stop working. With rising costs, this may not be enough to pay for food, a place to live and health care. About one-seventh of the people over 65 are at the poverty level. It is very hard for them to earn more money. There is even a limit on the amount of money they can earn (up to age 72) and still receive their full Social Security payment.

The third big problem faced by people over 65 is loneliness. In 1960 about 3 million old people lived alone. By 1978 it was almost 7 million. The people who say they are the loneliest are those who have recently lost a husband or wife. At a time when their spouses and friends are dying and leaving them alone, society makes life for the elderly worse. It tells them they cannot work. It tells them they cannot contribute anymore because they are too old.

Hospitals and nursing homes have been seen as a way to care for the elderly. But only about .4% of the elderly in this country live in hospitals or nursing homes. These places often seem to worsen the problems felt by old people. Most old people in nursing homes have no living relatives. More than 80% are below the poverty level. If they could get proper care and support, 30% to 60% of the old people in nursing homes could live in the community.

Although old people have many problems, their lives are easier than old people's lives in the past. The number of years a person lives has increased. A baby born in 1900 was expected to live about 47 years. A baby born today can expect to live about 71 years. Doctors can better help with the health problems of old age. Behavioral scientists are studying the problems of the elderly. Other people are beginning to look at how society sees old people and cares for them. All of this should one day make living to an old age safer, healthier and easier.

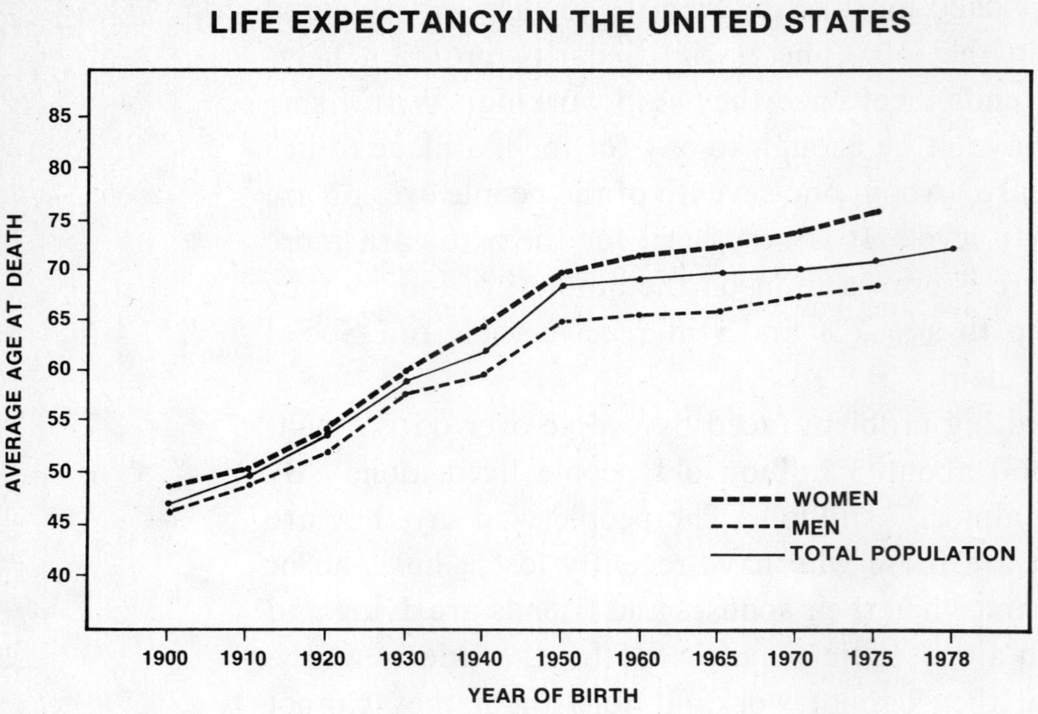

21. As the number of old people goes up, the main result is that
______(1) it is harder for them to use trains and buses
______(2) more is being learned about their special problems
______(3) they must retire at age 65 or 70
______(4) they get sick easily
______(5) more and more of them are living alone

22. A baby born in 1900 could at that time expect to live to the age of
______(1) 47
______(2) 71
______(3) 65
______(4) less than five years
______(5) 80

23. This passage implies that
______(1) all old people are poor and should be given more Social Security
______(2) older people have no serious problems
______(3) life for old people might be better if society changed its thinking about old age
______(4) more old people should live in old-age homes where they can get better care
______(5) people who are old should not try to go out

24. Which of the following would NOT help solve any of the problems discussed in this passage?
    ______(1) lowering the retirement age to 55
    ______(2) letting older people take part in classroom volunteer programs in elementary schools
    ______(3) starting more afternoon lunch programs for old people
    ______(4) bringing visiting nurses to old people in small towns
    ______(5) teaching bus and train operators about old people's problems

25. The field of gerontology
    ______(1) will be less important in the future
    ______(2) encourages a lower retirement age
    ______(3) should have no effect on government and social programs
    ______(4) will have more and more importance as the elderly population grows
    ______(5) is concerned with the needs of young children

Answers begin on page 139.

BEHAVIORAL SCIENCE PASSAGE 6

KEY WORDS

unconscious—(adjective) having to do with the part of the mind or a cause of behavior that a person is not fully aware of; (noun) the unconscious part of the mind

defense mechanism—(noun) a way of thinking or acting that the mind uses to protect itself from anxiety; repression is one defense mechanism

anxiety—(noun) a feeling of fear, worry and nervousness about what may happen

Sigmund Freud was one of the most important scientists to add to what we know in modern psychology. He first studied medicine and became a doctor. But his interest in understanding the human mind pushed him more and more into the field of psychology. He believed that by studying people—how they feel, what they do, and what they think—he could explain how the mind works.

One of Freud's main ideas was that the mind has conscious and unconscious parts. Some behaviors and feelings are conscious. This means a person knows why he or she does or feels something. What is in the conscious part of the mind is what a person is aware of or understands.

Other behaviors and feelings are unconscious. The person doesn't know why he or she does or feels something. The reasons the person gives or thinks, said Freud, may not be the true reasons.

Freud was not the first person to talk about the unconscious. He was the first to stress its importance. Much of his work was an attempt to describe the unconscious mind.

Freud said that the conscious part of the mind controls and holds down or represses some thoughts and feelings. It keeps these unconscious. Repression, he said, is one of our defense mechanisms. The mind uses defense mechanisms to protect itself from feelings of anxiety. It protects us from things we don't want to feel or think about. These ideas, then, are held in the unconscious part of the mind.

Freud felt that even the healthy mind needs to be protected by defense mechanisms. He thought that mental illness, though, could be caused when people repressed frightening, unhappy events from their childhoods. He said that if these repressed memories could be worked on and brought back to the conscious part of the mind, mentally ill people could be cured.

Much of Freud's work had to do with finding ways to help people deal with unconscious thoughts. At first he tried hypnotizing people. He thought that this would be an easy way for the person to talk about repressed thoughts. But he found that some people could not be hypnotized. He began to try another method called free association. Here, he would simply help the person talk freely by letting one idea lead to another. Later he even studied dreams and tried to understand their meanings.

There are many who do not agree with what Freud thought. His work has been widely studied. The things he tried have become the most common ways to treat some forms of mental illness and to understand human behavior. These are some of the many reasons for Freud's importance in behavioral science.

26. This passage mainly describes Freud's work with understanding
   ______(1) free association
   ______(2) hypnosis
   ______(3) medicine
   ______(4) the conscious and unconscious
   ______(5) dreams

27. Freud used free association because not all people
   ______(1) like to dream
   ______(2) can be hypnotized
   ______(3) are mentally ill
   ______(4) have a conscious mind
   ______(5) have an unconscious mind

28. From what you read, you could say that paying attention to dreams may
   ______(1) put a person under a sort of hypnosis
   ______(2) help make a person unconscious
   ______(3) create repression
   ______(4) have nothing to do with the study of psychology
   ______(5) help a person remember repressed thoughts or feelings

29. You can infer from the passage that the idea of the unconscious
   ______(1) existed before Freud described it
   ______(2) was unknown to Freud
   ______(3) didn't develop until after Freud died
   ______(4) has no truth to it
   ______(5) was much too hard to be studied

30. Freud's work
   ______(1) was not put into books until the last few years
   ______(2) has only been used by a few people
   ______(3) is accepted today by all behavorial scientists
   ______(4) has added much to what we think about the mind
   ______(5) is accepted today by everyone

Answers begin on page 140.

ANSWERS AND EXPLANATIONS—BEHAVIORAL SCIENCE

1. **(3)** is the best way to state the main idea of Passage 1. The passage is about the three major fields of behavioral science—psychology, sociology and anthropology. None of the other choices gives the full picture.

2. **(4)** sociology is the study of groups. This is one of the facts used to explain the main idea.

3. **(1)** an anthropology book might tell you something about Eskimo religions. Anthropology is the study of cultures. Religious beliefs are part of what culture means.

4. **(2)** is the only answer that is true. It is the only answer that can be inferred from the passage.

5. **(5)** is the answer that best describes the goals of behavioral science.

6. **(3)** is correct. The whole passage talks about marriage as an institution in most societies. Marriage customs differ from society to society but the institution of marriage always fills important needs in society.

7. **(4)** is correct. Find this answer in the next to the last paragraph.

8. **(2)** is correct. The dowry is money and gifts a woman's parents give her husband-to-be. Since a modern American wedding is usually paid for by the bride's parents, this is somewhat like the dowry.

9. **(1)** is correct. The passage talks about the bride's price, a custom where the man had to pay a woman's family to marry. It follows that a poor man might not be able to pay this price.

10. **(5)** is correct. This is the conclusion of the passage. The other choices are either false, or opinions that you cannot say the writer has.

11. **(3)** is the best answer. The passage defines conformity and what is good and bad about it. It focuses, however, on the experiment that shows how a person's ideas can be influenced by what people around him or her think.

12. **(2)** is correct. This detail about how the experiment was done can be found in the fourth paragraph of the passage.

13. **(3)** is the best answer. The passage states that people are often influenced by what others think and do. You can apply that fact to answer this question about voting.

14. **(5)** is most likely what the person would do. In the experiment about one-third of the people actually gave the wrong answer to be like the group. In real life most people go along with expected behavior or with what people around them are doing.

15. **(5)** is the best conclusion to make here. Conformity cannot be thought of as all good or all bad.

16. **(5)** is the only correct answer. This is a good way to state the main idea of the passage.

17. **(4)** is the correct answer. Find the numbers that give you this information in paragraph five.

18. **(3)** is the correct answer. You can apply what the passage says about the broader social changes coming from changes in women's social roles to the case here. Because social roles for people are tied closely to each other, a change in one will mean changes in many other areas.

19. **(2)** is the correct answer. It is the only idea that can be inferred from the passage. The other answers are not true. Although some people believe (5) is true. (5) ignores other factors that change and disrupt family life.

20. **(5)** is the correct answer. Changing social roles are not isolated events. The changes affect many areas of society. The other answers are not true, or not necessarily true.

21. **(2)** is the correct answer. None of the other choices is the main result of increasing numbers of old people as stated in the passage.

22. **(1)** is the correct answer. The last paragraph tells you this.

23. **(3)** is the correct answer. The passage focuses on the importance of knowing more about the problems of the elderly. It implies that greater knowledge will make life for the elderly better.

24. **(1)** is the only choice that would not be of any help in solving the problems of older people. All the other choices sound like good ideas.

25. **(4)** is the correct answer. The other answers are not true. From all that is said in the passage, you can conclude that gerontology will become more important as our population ages.

26. **(4)** is the correct answer. The others are related details of Freud's study of the conscious and unconscious parts of the mind.

27. **(2)** is the correct answer. You should remember this fact from the passage.

28. **(5)** is the correct answer. Paragraph seven says that Freud used dreams, along with free association and hypnosis to help patients remember thoughts and feelings that were repressed. Therefore, it follows that paying attention to dreams may be helpful in doing that.

29. **(1)** is the correct answer. You can infer that this is so since we are told that he was not the first person to talk about the unconscious.

30. **(4)** is the correct answer. The last paragraph concludes that not everyone agrees with Freud, but his work has become one of the most common ways to treat mental illness and understand behavior.

POST-TEST

Directions: **The Post-Test is made up of 35 questions from economics, geography, political science, history and behavioral science. Some questions follow a reading passage. They are like those you worked on in this book. Read each of these passages. Then answer the questions from what you read. Other questions stand alone. Use your own experience or prior knowledge to answer these questions. Still other questions come after a cartoon, a graph or a chart. Answer these questions after studying the cartoon, graph or chart.**

There is no time limit. If you don't know an answer, try to figure it out. You can even guess at some answers. Read all five choices. Then put a check mark (✓) next to the BEST answer for each question.

When you finish answering the 35 questions, check your answers with the Answers and Explanations that follow. Circle each correct answer. Then fill in the Post-Test Skill Record on page 162. Compare your Post-Test results with what you did on the Pre-Test. Look for the reading skills that need more work. Plan to strengthen these as you go on in your studies.

Sociology is a field of behavioral science. It deals with how society works. It studies people as members of groups. Some studies in sociology look at one society as a whole. Others compare different social systems of the world.

Some areas of sociology involve studies of social habits, population trends or group behaviors. Sociology is also the study of social change. Some sociologists view their role as raising the level of what people know about social forces. Others stress helping people solve problems. Still others see themselves mainly as social researchers.

Most sociologists agree that their field has two broad goals. Its first goal is to show the social order as it is. The second is to increase our understanding of society in order to change our world for the better.

1. A sociologist would be LEAST concerned with
   ______(1) how people behave in groups
   ______(2) why there are diseases in the world
   ______(3) how societies change
   ______(4) how people learn social habits
   ______(5) how groups of people adjust to city life

2. As the world population grows, sociologists
   ______(1) become all the more important
   ______(2) must stick to the old views
   ______(3) will not be able to find new ways to meet world needs
   ______(4) will become less and less important
   ______(5) may solve health problems

"To the victor go the spoils." This saying has some truth in politics as well as in war. The spoils system is the practice of giving government jobs to those who worked for the successful political party or candidate. Sometimes this is called a patronage system. The jobs may be given without regard for the person's skills or experience. They are merely rewards for doing the political work that helped win an election.

3. A chief problem with the patronage system is that
   ______(1) not all party workers can be hired
   ______(2) it offers no long-term job security
   ______(3) people with little skill may be given key jobs
   ______(4) not all U.S. politicians use it
   ______(5) no one is sure which party will win

---

4. The warning about smoking
   ______(1) is required by law on cigarette packages
   ______(2) must be posted in all public places
   ______(3) is a slogan of the American Medical Association
   ______(4) is not approved by the U.S. government
   ______(5) is not true

Copyright 1977 by Herblock in *The Washington Post*

5. The cartoonist feels that the actions of the left hand and the right hand

______(1) make voters happy
______(2) are both dangerous, but he's not sure which one is worse
______(3) show that the left hand should keep adding money to tobacco programs
______(4) are both actions that are needed
______(5) are in conflict with each other

By the 1840s Americans felt that the United States had an important job to do. The young country felt it had what was called a "divine mission." Many Americans saw two tasks in this special, or god-given, mission. One was to push the boundaries of this country all the way to the Pacific Ocean. The other was to build a very strong system of personal freedom. They wanted a system so strong that other nations would never be able to take away the American right to self-government. Americans came to call this divine mission their "Manifest Destiny." It became one more reason for the country to grow and develop itself into a powerful nation.

6. The term "Manifest Destiny" meant that America
   ______(1) had a new kind of government
   ______(2) was fearful of other nations
   ______(3) had no right to self-government
   ______(4) was clearly meant to work toward certain goals
   ______(5) was a great democracy

---

7. The name or symbol used by people or companies to set their goods apart from those made by others is a
   ______(1) fair trade item
   ______(2) copyright
   ______(3) quota
   ______(4) trademark
   ______(5) cartel

American workers began forming labor unions in the late 1700s. At that time many of them worked up to 18 hours a day in factories. Workers were often packed into dark, dirty workrooms. Low wages forced most of them to live in crowded, unhealthy slums. Workers decided to fight for higher wages and better working conditions.

The first unions were local groups of skilled craftsmen such as printers, carpenters or shoemakers. Through strikes and bloody fights with bosses, they won job improvements and higher pay.

By the 1880s, many of these small craft locals found they could gain even more power by joining with others to form a national union of all crafts. The American Federation of Labor (A.F.L.) was born in 1886.

By 1920 over four million workers belonged to the A.F.L. In the 1930s, the Great Depression caused layoffs and wage cuts. Millions of workers across the country went on strike in protest.

While the A.F.L. helped improve life for craft workers, it did little for workers on assembly lines or in big factories. The Congress of Industrial Organizations (C.I.O.) was formed in 1935 to help these workers.

The C.I.O. represented all working people, not just skilled craftsmen. It also pushed the government to start programs like unemployment insurance, Social Security and welfare.

For the next 20 years, the C.I.O. and the A.F.L. fought each other for new members. Finally, in 1955, the two joined into one large organization. Since then, the A.F.L.-C.I.O. has helped its members win better wages and more government protection. Some people say that the A.F.L.-C.I.O. is not doing enough for workers. These people feel that strikes would win more for workers than deals made between union leaders and management. Others say the A.F.L.-C.I.O. is not trying to organize the growing number of minority and women workers.

No one is sure what the future of the labor movement will be. But problems and disagreements between labor and management show that unions are still needed to protect the rights of workers.

8. From the passage you can conclude that

______(1) with no unions, conditions would be poor for workers
______(2) unions will solve all labor problems
______(3) world-wide unions will be formed
______(4) unions are growing too fast
______(5) the A.F.L.-C.I.O. is bad for working people

9. The last paragraph of the passage suggests that
   ______(1) conflict between labor and management will soon end
   ______(2) more unions are needed
   ______(3) unions do nothing for working people
   ______(4) war may soon be fought over labor problems
   ______(5) conflict will continue between labor and management

10. The main idea of the passage concerns
    ______(1) the organizations that workers formed to protect their interests
    ______(2) the growth of local unions in America
    ______(3) the history of America's industrial growth
    ______(4) how the A.F.L. joined forces with the C.I.O.
    ______(5) the first labor laws in America

In a free economic system, what people buy can have a direct effect on how much they have to pay and how much is produced. Buying habits can force prices up if what people want is in short supply. On the other hand, if buying is slow and supplies are up, stores may slash prices and find other ways to make people buy more. As much as possible, goods are produced and sold at a rate that matches the demand for them. This is how the law of supply and demand works. A balance between supplies of goods and consumer demand keeps prices steady.

11. According to the law of supply and demand which headline would LEAST affect prices?
    ______(1) Severe Hail Storm Destroys Florida Orange Crop
    ______(2) Heat Wave Brings Rise In City Crime Rate
    ______(3) Huge Oil Field Discovered In Alaska
    ______(4) American Birthrate Drops Sharply
    ______(5) Strike Closes 300 Plywood Factories

12. The passage says that the law of supply and demand means that
    ______(1) consumer buying habits rarely affect prices
    ______(2) prices never affect what people buy
    ______(3) when an item becomes scarce, its price drops

_____(4) when prices go down, people stop buying

_____(5) consumers can sometimes affect prices and production

---

CHART 1

As various ethnic groups become part of a society and different cultures meet, two things may happen:

1. Contacts among people and groups can enrich all the cultures. New ideas and customs are gained by all.
2. Fear and distrust can prevent sharing and can keep people from changing. The result will be conflict and social problems.

The United States has long been called a "melting pot" of ethnic groups. Chart 1 shows numbers of refugees admitted from 1977 to 1980. Chart 2 "Wave of New Americans" lists all immigrants, not just refugees. It compares totals from the years 1965 and 1978.

WAVE OF NEW AMERICANS			
1978		1965	
Country of Birth	How Many	Country of Birth	How Many
Mexico	92,367	Canada	38,326
Vietnam	88,543	Mexico	37,969
Philippines	37,216	Great Britain	27,358
Cuba	29,754	Germany	24,045
Korea	29,288	Cuba	19,760
China, Taiwan	21,315	Colombia	10,885
India	20,753	Italy	10,821
Dominican Republic	19,458	Dominican Republic	9,504
Jamaica	19,265	Poland	8,465
Canada	16,863	Argentina	6,124
Great Britain	14,245	Ireland	5,463
Colombia	11,032	Ecuador	4,392
Portugal	10,445	China, Taiwan	4,057
Guyana	7,614	France	4,039
Italy	7,415	Haiti	3,609
From other countries	175,869	From other countries	81,879
TOTAL	**601,442**	**TOTAL**	**296,697**

CHART 2

13. According to chart 1, the number of refugees admitted to America from 1977 to 1980

______(1) added up to about one million
______(2) increased by 50,000 each year
______(3) tripled every year
______(4) did not increase as years went by
______(5) kept increasing each year

14. Chart 2 shows that the number of Mexican immigrants was

______(1) larger in 1965 than in 1978
______(2) higher than all other groups when the two years are added together
______(3) higher than all other groups in both 1965 and 1978
______(4) less than the total number coming from Cuba, Argentina and Ecuador
______(5) more than half the total of all immigrants

15. Many immigrants settle in California. One reason may be that

_____(1) it is the largest state in the United States
_____(2) people must go through California to enter the United States
_____(3) the warm climate is similar to their home climates
_____(4) California has a lot of cheap farmland
_____(5) it is in the center of the United States

16. How does the writer say that the different ethnic groups get along in the United States? The writer

_____(1) does not give an opinion
_____(2) says that all groups are learning about each other
_____(3) fears conflict soon
_____(4) says that there are too many new groups
_____(5) states that America has a moral duty to be a melting pot

---

17. America changed from a farm to an industrial economy shortly after

_____(1) the American Revolution
_____(2) the War of 1812
_____(3) the Civil War
_____(4) the start of the 20th century
_____(5) 1930

Members of social groups understand, accept and share a set of rules about their behavior. These rules are called norms. Norms are standards of behavior. Norms in a social group or society develop over time. As a behavior keeps filling people's needs, it becomes the norm, or normal way of acting. Patterns of dating, marriage customs, how children are raised and how people act on their jobs are just some of the behavior patterns that are based on norms.

18. Which quote shows the most concern about going along with norms?
    ______(1) "Let me do my own thing."
    ______(2) "But what will the neighbors say?"
    ______(3) "It's my body and I'll do as I please."
    ______(4) "Laws are made to be broken."
    ______(5) "Who cares what others think!"

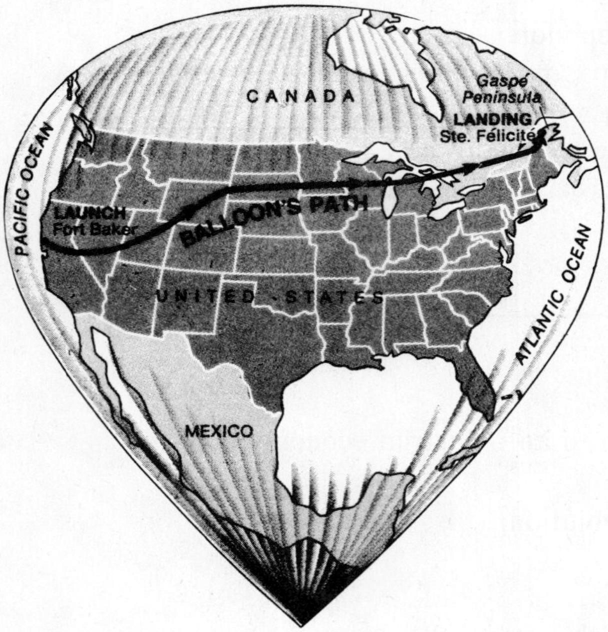

19. The map shows the route of a balloon. You can see that its path
    ______(1) was from north to south
    ______(2) was never in Canada
    ______(3) crossed one ocean
    ______(4) crossed much of the northern United States
    ______(5) began in Mexico

Social Security is a national insurance plan. It gives unemployment benefits and old-age pensions to those who have been wage earners in the United States. Workers and their employers give to the fund. In theory, each worker's money is set aside for his or her own benefits. During unemployment, in time of long illness, or when a worker retires, Social Security benefits are paid.

In practice, the money taken from today's worker is used for those who need Social Security benefits now. It follows that someone else's payments will help to pay benefits for today's workers when they need them.

In recent years, life expectancy has increased. As more people live longer, demands for Social Security benefits have grown faster than funds to meet those demands. This is an example of a system that must change to keep up with the times.

20. From the passage the term "life expectancy" seems to mean

______(1) Social Security problems
______(2) expected unemployment benefits
______(3) retirement age of most people
______(4) length of time people generally live
______(5) payments made during one's life

21. Unless the Social Security system is changed, the passage concludes that

______(1) people may stop taking part in it
______(2) it will have to refund payments made in the past
______(3) benefits may vary with inflation
______(4) it may run out of funds
______(5) it will build up too much money

---

22. An immigrant is a person who comes to settle permanently in a country other than his or her own. How is a refugee different from such a person? A refugee

______(1) leaves his or her native land for only a brief time
______(2) enters a foreign country to escape danger
______(3) has strong religious views
______(4) buys land in a foreign nation
______(5) takes part in a revolution

23. The belief that any ethnic group, other than one's own, has low intelligence, strange ways or poor styles of living is

_____(1) criticism
_____(2) prejudice
_____(3) ranking
_____(4) nationalism
_____(5) patriotism

Public opinion can help shape policies made by our leaders. In America, by law, people have the right to state their views and to hear the views of others. This exchange of ideas leads to intelligent voting.

But fewer and fewer people vote each year in the United States. Many claim they no longer trust politicians. Others say that candidates represent only the interests of the rich and powerful.

If people want control over their government, they must stand up for what they believe. They must vote, and they must demand that their needs be met. Only then can they hope to affect public policy.

24. The writer says that public opinion

_____(1) has no real power in politics
_____(2) creates problems for candidates
_____(3) is often wrong and must be checked
_____(4) can play a key role in American government
_____(5) should not be part of our system

The International Court of Justice was set up to help solve problems between nations. In 1945, the World Court, an arm of the United Nations, replaced the International Court of Justice.

The World Court counts on the goodwill of nations to enforce its findings. It has no police force or prison system to carry out its ideas. No nation can be forced to accept the judgments of the court. Because of this, many feel that the court is worthless.

One job of the World Court is to interpret treaties between nations. It also deals with problems which could cause international trouble. The 15 justices of the court are chosen by the General Assembly and the Security Council of the United Nations. They must all come from different member nations. Each justice serves on the court for nine years.

25. The only reason nations might obey the World Court's rulings is that

______(1) it has power to declare war
______(2) it is backed by a world police force
______(3) it can enforce trade embargoes
______(4) it was set up by the United States
______(5) it is respected as an agent of goodwill

26. How many justices make up the World Court?

______(1) one from each member of the United Nations
______(2) 1945
______(3) 15
______(4) it depends on the number of cases
______(5) 12

---

27. When representatives of labor and management meet to settle a disagreement it is called

______(1) federal law
______(2) the union shop
______(3) legal rulings
______(4) collective bargaining
______(5) court orders

"Our token Black - is that really how you think of yourself, Ms Corwin? You're much more than that, I assure you. You're also our token woman."

28. The cartoon suggests that
______(1) the woman is the group leader
______(2) the men do not like having a female board member
______(3) the woman—as a black person *and* a woman—makes it seem that no groups are left out
______(4) women's rights are equal to men's
______(5) black people have good jobs

29. The country with the largest land area in the world is
______(1) The United States of America
______(2) Nationalist China
______(3) The Union of Soviet Socialist Republics
______(4) Brazil
______(5) Asia

Africa is the largest of the three southern continents of the world. It is made up of many countries and covers more than 11 million square miles. This is about 20% of all the land on Earth.

The countries of Africa have had a long, rich history. For more than 200 years, however, European powers have tried to control the continent. Parts of Africa have been claimed at one time or another by France, England, Italy, Germany, and other nations. Most of these nations have tried to force their culture, religion and way of life on the people of Africa. They saw Africa as a land of rich natural resources and raw materials.

Three main groups of people have lived in the southern part of the African continent. The Bushmen were the first people to live there. They were small, sturdy hunters and gatherers who did not farm. Later the Hottentots brought in a more advanced culture. They spread further south than the Bushmen. The Hottentots were living at the most southern tip of Africa when explorers from Europe arrived. The Bantus were the most recent people of southern Africa. Their culture was even further advanced. The Bantu people farmed and herded cattle. The Zulu tribe is perhaps the most well-known of the Bantu people.

When white explorers came to southern Africa, life changed. These changes, along with wars, destroyed the native culture of the Bushmen and Hottentots. The Bantu way of life was upset, though many of these people still live in the region. Africa is a vast continent with a long history and many different cultural groups.

30. The writer suggests that the coming of white explorers

______(1) saved Africa's economy
______(2) was too late to save the culture
______(3) harmed the tribal cultures
______(4) brought health laws to help Africa
______(5) ended old tribal wars

31. Africa is

_____(1) the smallest continent on Earth
_____(2) smaller than Australia
_____(3) the same size as South America
_____(4) smaller than South America
_____(5) larger than South America

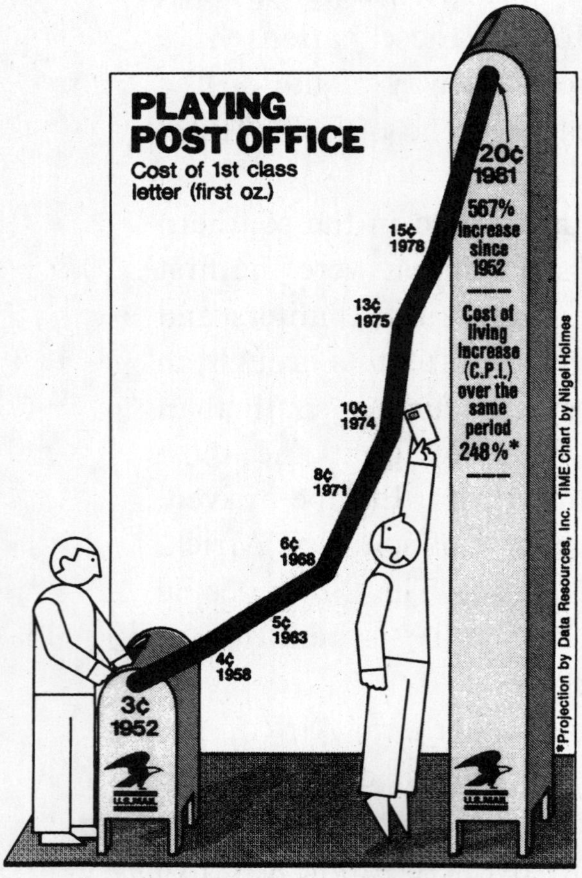

The picture shows that the cost of postage went up 567%. During the same time, the C.P.I went up 248%.

32. C.P.I. stands for

_____(1) Complete Price Increase
_____(2) Cost Per Individual
_____(3) Cost Price Indicator
_____(4) Consumer Price Index
_____(5) Cash Price Index

The world's water supply is one of our chief natural resources. The earth's water can be divided into ground water and surface water. Oceans are considered ground water because they are deep and permanent. Surface water comes in the form of lakes, rivers, streams, and ponds. These are not permanent features but can dry up or change course for a variety of reasons. This does not mean that surface water is unimportant. It is basic to the survival of most living things.

Surface water can change the landscape. The Grand Canyon was formed by the Colorado River. The force of this river carved a gorge which is now one mile deep and more than 200 miles long. The force of running water washed away the soil. It also cut through solid rock.

We use water and its power daily. Examples of this are dams, canals, water turbines, and irrigation systems. In our technical world, as well as in the natural world, water is a key resource.

33. The main point stated about water is that it

______(1) can be polluted
______(2) is in limited supply
______(3) is necessary for life
______(4) can wash away soil and rock
______(5) has some technical uses

34. Since the oceans are considered ground water, we may expect that they

______(1) will not dry up
______(2) cannot be polluted
______(3) are not affected by humans
______(4) are less important than lakes
______(5) are slowly getting smaller

35. A gorge is

______(1) a river or stream
______(2) an inland sea
______(3) a measure of water power
______(4) part of a canal
______(5) a gap or valley cut by water

ANSWERS AND EXPLANATIONS—POST-TEST

Inference 1. **(2)** is correct. This is one area probably not studied in sociology. The passage tells you that sociology deals with people in societies and in groups. You can figure out that all of the other answers have something to do with that.

Conclusion 2. **(1)** is correct. The growing population means there will be more groups and more interaction among people. You can conclude that the study of sociology will gain in importance.

Application 3. **(3)** is the best answer. The others may be true, but (3) gives the problem that might do the most harm.

Prior Knowledge 4. **(1)** is the best answer. The warning about smoking is required by law. Otherwise, it would not be mentioned in connection with spending government money on tobacco programs.

Inference 5. **(5)** is the best answer. The expressions on the men's faces and the actions of the man's left and right hands imply a conflict.

Inference 6. **(4)** is correct. You can figure this out from the statement that the U.S. had a divine mission and task.

Prior Knowledge 7. **(4)** is the best answer. Individual artists or makers of goods have their own trademarks.

Conclusion 8. **(1)** is the correct answer. The passage tells about bad conditions that existed before unions. Throughout the passage, the writer shows how unions have helped workers.

Inference 9. **(5)** is the best answer. The last sentence says that unions are still fighting to help workers. You can infer from this that conflict will probably continue.

Main Idea 10. (**1**) is correct. All of the other choices are details that relate to the main idea.

Application 11. (**2**) is the best answer. It would have the least effect on prices. All of the other choices have more far-reaching effects related to supply and demand.

Detail 12. (**5**) is correct. This is stated in the passage.

Detail 13. (**5**) is correct. In the four years, the number of refugees went from 32,000 to 234,200 by increasing each year.

Detail 14. (**2**) is correct. All of the other choices are false.

Application 15. (**3**) is the best answer. You can see that many of the immigrants came from warm countries. It is reasonable that they would prefer a warm, sunny state. Also, the other choices are not true.

Detail 16. (**1**) is correct. If you read carefully, you saw that the writer states possible happenings, but does not say what he thinks will happen.

Prior Knowledge 17. (**3**) is the best answer. America was industrialized after the Civil War.

Application 18. (**2**) is the best answer. Norms relate to doing what a person is expected to do.

Application 19. (**4**) is the correct answer. By following the path marked on the map, you can see that the balloon started in California and traveled across the northern part of the U.S.

Inference 20. (**4**) is the correct answer. In the last paragraph it says: "As more people live longer. . . ."

Conclusion 21. (**4**) is the best answer. The writer states in the last paragraph that demands have grown faster than the funds. Need for change is mentioned in the last sentence.

Prior Knowledge	22.	**(2)** is the best answer. (1), (3), (4) and (5) may be true but are not necessarily true of refugees.
Prior Knowledge	23.	**(2)** is the correct answer. Prejudice against any group of people comes from a lack of information and understanding of a culture other than one's own.
Main Idea	24.	**(4)** is the correct answer. The writer states this at the beginning and end of the passage.
Conclusion	25.	**(5)** is the correct answer. The passage says that the court counts on goodwill. It says that it was started by the United Nations. (5) is the right conclusion to make.
Detail	26.	**(3)** is correct. It is stated in the last paragraph.
Prior Knowledge	27.	**(4)** is the correct answer.
Inference	28.	**(3)** is correct. You can figure this out by the use of the term "token woman" and "token black."
Prior Knowledge	29.	**(3)** is the correct answer.
Inference	30.	**(3)** is the best answer. The writer refers to wars and changes that destroyed or upset tribal cultures.
Application	31.	**(5)** is correct. You can figure this out from the first line of the passage if you know which are northern and which are southern continents.
Prior Knowledge	32.	**(4)** is the correct answer.
Main Idea	33.	**(3)** is correct. It is stated at the beginning and at the end of the passage.
Inference	34.	**(1)** is correct. The use of the word permanent in talking about the oceans implies this.

Inference 35. **(5)** is correct. You can figure this out from the passage. It tells that the Colorado River carved a gorge which is now one mile deep and more than 200 miles long.

POST-TEST ANSWER KEY

1. **(2)**	8. **(1)**	15. **(3)**	22. **(2)**	29. **(3)**
2. **(1)**	9. **(5)**	16. **(1)**	23. **(2)**	30. **(3)**
3. **(3)**	10. **(1)**	17. **(3)**	24. **(4)**	31. **(5)**
4. **(1)**	11. **(2)**	18. **(2)**	25. **(5)**	32. **(4)**
5. **(5)**	12. **(5)**	19. **(4)**	26. **(3)**	33. **(3)**
6. **(4)**	13. **(5)**	20. **(2)**	27. **(4)**	34. **(1)**
7. **(4)**	14. **(2)**	21. **(4)**	28. **(3)**	35. **(5)**

POST-TEST SKILL RECORD

Directions: Fill in the Post-Test Skill Record after you have taken the Post-Test and have checked your answers. The Skill Record will show your strengths in social studies reading skills and prior knowledge. Turn back to the Pre-Test Skill Record to compare your scores.

POST-TEST DATE: ______________________

Post-Test Skills	Total Questions	Test Questions	Number Correct
• Finding the Main Idea	3	10,24,33	
• Recalling Details	5	12,13, 14,16,26	
• Applying Facts and Ideas	6	3,11, 15,18,19,31	
• Making Inferences	9	1,5,6,9,20, 28,30,34,35	
• Drawing Conclusions	4	2,8,21,25	
• Using Prior Knowledge	8	4,7,17,22, 23,27,29,32	
TOTAL	**35**	**TEST SCORE**	

GLOSSARY

The following glossary can serve as a helpful study aid. It explains all of the key words plus lots of other unusual or difficult words from the reading passages. The listings in parentheses after each definition tell you where that word is used in the book.

—A—

accuse—(verb) to charge someone with doing something wrong (Political Science #5)

advantage—(noun) something that gives extra help to a situation (History #5, #6)

aged—(adjective) old (Behavioral Science #5)

ally—(noun) a friend; a country that joins with another country to achieve some goal (History #6)

amendment—(noun) a change; especially a change in the Constitution (Political Science #3, #5)

anthropology—(noun) the study of culture (Behavioral Science #1)

anxiety—(noun) a feeling of fear, worry and nervousness about what may happen (Behavioral Science #6)

appoint—(verb) to choose someone for a high-level government position (Political Science #2)

authority—(noun) the power or right to act or make decisions (Political Science #4)

Axis power—(noun) Germany, Italy or Japan—a country that joined to fight the Allied powers in World War II (History #6)

—B—

backward—(adjective) at a low level of development; ignorant (History #5)

bail—(noun) money paid to release a prisoner until the day of his or her trial; the money guarantees that the prisoner will return for trial (Political Science #5)

balance of trade—(noun) the difference over a period of time between what a country spends on imports and what it earns on exports (Economics #4)

ballot—(noun) a piece of paper used by a voter in an election to mark the candidate of his or her choice (Political Science #6)

barter—(noun) a system of trading goods and services without using money (Economics #6)

behavior—(noun) how a person or thing behaves or acts (Geography #1; Behavioral Science #1, #2, #3, #4, #6)

birth control—(noun) a way to control the number of children being born; some methods used are the birth control pill, intrauterine device (IUD), diaphragm, condom, and abortion (Geography #6)

bondage—(noun) slavery; lack of freedom (History #3)

—C—

candidate—(noun) someone trying to get elected to a political office (Political Science #6)

capital goods—(noun) factories, tools and machines used to make things to sell (Economics #5)

capitalism—(noun) an economic system in which certain persons or groups own land, factories and other means of producing goods; they compete against one another to earn a profit (Economics #5)

capitalist—(noun) a person who owns some type of capital goods (Economics #5)

cartographer—(noun) a person who makes and studies maps (Geography #2)

checks and balances, system of—(noun) the system set up to make sure that each branch of the federal government does what it is supposed to; each branch watches and checks actions of the other branches (Political Science #2)

circulation—(noun) the movement of money from one person to another (Economics #1)

citizen—(noun) a person living in a country and guaranteed protection by that country's government (Political Science #3)

civil—(adjective) something relating to citizens (Political Science #3)

civil law—(noun) the law dealing with private rights of individuals and businesses (Political Science #4)

civil right—(noun) a right that belongs to a person because he or she lives in a state or country (Political Science #3)

climate—(noun) the average weather conditions of a place—temperature, rainfall, humidity and wind conditions, for example (Geography #1, #4)

colonist—(noun) a person living in a colony (History #2)

colony—(noun) a group of people who settle in a new place but keep ties to their homeland (Economics #6; History #2, #5)

common law—(noun) the law based on past court cases or custom (Political Science #4)

communism—(noun) an economic and political system in which land, factories and other means of producing goods are owned in common (Economics #5)

confess—(verb) to admit doing something wrong (Political Science #5)

conflict—(noun) a fight or disagreement (Political Science #1)
(verb) to strongly disagree (Political Science #4)

conformity—(noun) following the rules; acting as your society or group expects you to (Behavioral Science #3)

Congress—(noun) the law-making branch of the U.S. government; Congress is made up of the Senate and the House of Representatives (Economics #2; Political Science #2, #3, #4, #6)

conquer—(verb) to gain or win over by force (Geography #4)

conscious—(adjective) having to do with the part of the mind or a cause of behavior that we are fully aware of (Behavioral Science #6)

Constitution—(noun) the basic written law of the U.S. government (Political Science #1, #2, #3, #4, #5)

constitutional—(adjective) legal according to the Constitution (Political Science #4)

consumer—(noun) a buyer or user of goods and services (Economics #1, #3)

continent—(noun) one of the seven large bodies of land on Earth (Geography #5)

contribute—(verb) to give something or to be involved in something (Behavioral Science #5)

corporation—(noun) a group of people joined to form a business organization with special legal rights (Economics #5)

cruelty—(noun) a cruel or mean action that causes pain and suffering (History #5)

culture—(noun) the way of life of a society; the society's knowledge, beliefs, art, morals, laws and customs (Geography #4, #5; Behavioral Science #1, #2)

currency—(noun) the money that a group of people use; dollars, quarters and dimes are part of the currency of the U.S. (Economics #6)

custom—(noun) an old belief; a traditional or useful way of doing something (Geography #3, #4; Behavioral Science #1, #2)

cycle—(noun) a series of events that repeats itself in the same order (Economics #3)

—D—

deduction—(noun) an amount that employers take out of their workers' paychecks for taxes, insurance or any other regular expenses (Economics #2)

defense mechanism—(noun) a way of thinking or acting that the mind uses to protect itself from anxiety (Behavioral Science #6)

define—(verb) to describe exactly (History #4)

degree—(noun) a unit of measurement (Geography #2)

deny—(verb) to refuse to give or allow (Political Science #3, #5; History #3)

depression—(noun) in economics, a time when business is very slow, production is cut back and many people are out of work (Economics #1; History #5, #6)

developed—(adjective) modern; in a developed country, most farms, factories, schools, hospitals, etc. use modern methods and machines (Geography #6)

discrimination—(noun) treating one group of people in an illegal or unfair way (Political Science #3; History #3)

dispute—(noun) an argument or disagreement (Geography #3; Political Science #4)

document—(noun) an official paper used as proof of something (History #1)

double jeopardy—(noun) being put on trial twice for the same crime (Political Science #5)

dowry—(noun) property that a woman gives to her husband at the time of their marriage (Behavioral Science #2)

due process of law—(noun) the correct and legal way that an arrest and a trial must be carried out (Political Science #5)

dwindle—(verb) to shrink slowly or become smaller (Economics #1)

—E—

economic system—(see economy)

economist—(noun) a person who studies economics and understands it very well (Economics #4)

economy—(noun) the part of human life dealing with making, passing out and using the goods and services in society; also known as an economic system (Economics #3, #4, #5; History #6)

elderly—(noun) an old person; the aged (adjective) old; aged (Behavioral Science #5)

elector—(noun) a person who is chosen to elect the president and vice-president of the United States (Political Science #6)

electoral college—(noun) the name given the whole body of electors (Political Science #6)

electoral vote—(noun) the total vote of the 538 electors (Political Science #6)

emperor—(noun) a man who rules a group of lands or countries known as an empire (Geography #5)

employee—(noun) a paid worker (Economics #2)

endow—(verb) to give something valuable (Political Science #4)

enforce—(verb) to make sure that a law is carried out (Political Science #2)

equator—(noun) an imaginary line around the earth, halfway between the north and south poles; the equator is known as 0° latitude (Geography #2)

ethnic group—(noun) a group of the same race or nationality whose members share traits and customs (Geography #5)

evaluate—(verb) to judge or decide the value of something (History #1)

exchange—(noun) trading one thing for another (Economics #4, #6)

executive branch—(noun) one of the three branches of the U.S. government; the executive branch consists of the president, his cabinet and related agencies (Political Science #2)

exist—(verb) to live or continue being (Behavioral Science #4)

expense—(noun) money spent on a necessary or useful item (Economics #2)

experiment—(noun) a test that is used to discover or prove something (Behavioral Science #3)

export—(noun) a product one nation sends to another nation (Economics #4)

—F—

Federal Insurance Contribution Act (F.I.C.A.)—(noun) the law setting up the Social Security system (Economics #2)

federalism—(noun) the sharing of power between states and a central government (Political Science #1, #2)

free market—(noun) an economic system in which the government has little or no control over prices and wages (Economics #5)

freedman—(noun) a black person freed from slavery after the Civil War (History #3)

forbid—(verb) to demand that something not be done (Political Science #3, #5)

foundation—(noun) something used as a base or support (Political Science #4)

—G—

gerontology—(noun) the study of aging and the problems of old people (Behavioral Science #5)

gold standard—(noun) an amount of gold set aside by the U.S. government to back up each dollar bill it prints (Economics #6)

goods—(noun) products or items for sale (Economics #1, #3, #4, #6; History #4, #5)

govern—(verb) to rule or control (Political Science #2; History #2)

government—(noun) the group or body that has the authority and power in a political unit to make and carry out laws and policies (Economics #2, #3, #4, #5, #6; Geography #3, #4, #5; Political Science #1, #2, #3, #4, #5, #6; History #1, #2, #3, #4, #5)

governor—(noun) the person elected to head a state (Geography #4)

grand jury—(noun) a group of citizens chosen to decide if an accused person should be put on trial (Political Science #5)

Grange, the—(noun) an organization of farmers formed in the late 1800s to protect themselves against unfair treatment by railroad companies (History #4)

grant—(verb) to give or allow (Political Science #3; History #3)

Great Depression—(noun) a period from 1929 through the early 1930s when the U.S. suffered its worst economic depression; banks and businesses across the country failed, leaving millions of people hungry and out of work (History #6)

—H—

high-yield—(adjective) high-producing (Geography #6)

historian—(noun) a person who studies and knows a lot about history (Economics #6; History #1)

hostile—(adjective) showing hate or anger; unfriendly (History #2)

House of Burgesses—(noun) the first self-governing group of colonists in the New World; it was made up of elected representatives from each plantation in Jamestown, Virginia (History #2)

humidity—(noun) water or moisture in the air (Geography #1)

—I—

immigrant—(noun) a person who leaves his or her home to settle in a new country (History #4)

impeach—(verb) to formally charge a public official with an illegal act (Political Science #2)

imperialism—(noun) spreading the power and wealth of a nation by taking over other lands (History #5)

import—(noun) a product brought into a country from another nation (Economics #4)

inalienable right—(noun) a person's right that cannot be legally taken away (Political Science #4)

indentured servant—(noun) a poor person who was brought to America during the colonial era; in exchange for his passage, the servant had to work for four to seven years without pay (History #2)

individual—(noun) one person
(adjective) one; separate (Behavioral Science #1)

industrialization—(noun) the growth of businesses and factories (History #4, #5)

industry—(noun) manufacturing plants and other businesses that produce things (Geography #4, #5)

inflation—(noun) a condition of the economy when there is more money and credit than goods and services; prices rise (Economics #1, #3; Political Science #2)

influence—(noun) the power to have an effect on something (History #2)

insight—(noun) a clear understanding of what makes something the way it is (Behavioral Science #1)

institution—(noun) a system of social roles and customs that serve an important need in the society (Behavioral Science #1, #2, #4)

interact—(verb) to act upon or have an effect on one another (Geography #1)

interfere—(verb) to disturb or get in the way of something (Political Science #2)

Internal Revenue Service (I.R.S.)—(noun) the government agency that collects taxes (Economics #2)

international trade—(noun) the exchange of goods and services between nations (Economics #4)

interpret—(verb) to explain or make clear (Political Science #4)

interpretation—(noun) an explanation; the act of explaining something (History #1)

—J—

Jim Crow law—(noun) a law or custom that treats black people unfairly or illegally (Political Science #3)

judicial branch—(noun) one of the three branches of the U.S. government; the judicial branch consists of the court system (Political Science #2)

—L—

latitude—(noun) distance measured in degrees on the surface of the earth from east to west; lines of latitude are called parallels (Geography #2)

law—(noun) a rule for behavior or action made and enforced by some authority or power (Political Science #4)

law of supply and demand—(noun) a basic law of economics that says value is related to how much of something is available (supply) and how many people want it (demand) (Economics #1)

legislature—(noun) a group of people who have been given the power to make laws (Geography #4; Political Science #4, #6)

legislative branch—(noun) one of the three branches of the U.S. government; the legislative branch consists of the lawmakers known as Congressmen (Political Science #2)

life expectancy—(noun) the number of years a person is likely to live (Geography #6)

longitude—(noun) distance measured in degrees on the surface of the earth from north to south; lines of longitude are called meridians (Geography #2)

—M—

majority—(noun) more than half of a group (Political Science #6)

market—(noun) demand for a product or the place to buy a product (History #4, #5)

marriage—(noun) a basic social institution that sets the way for two people to come together and build a lasting family unit (Behavioral Science #2)

marriage broker—(noun) a matchmaker; someone who arranges marriages for other people (Behavioral Science #2)

meridian—(noun) an imaginary line running from the north to south pole which marks longitude (Geography #2)

mestizo—(noun) a person of mixed Indian and Spanish background living in Mexico (Geography #4)

mindless—(adjective) without thinking; not using the mind (Behavioral Science #3)

mineral—(noun) a nonliving substance usually formed in the ground, such as coal, stone, or salt (Geography #1)

minority—(noun) a group of people with the same race, religion, nationality or political views who are different from most people in society (Geography #5)

monarchy—(noun) a country ruled by a king or queen (Geography #5)

monopoly—(noun) a company that controls all of the making or selling of an item or service (Economics #3)

morals—(noun) proper and honest actions or beliefs (Behavioral Science #1)

myth—(noun) an untrue story that many people believe and that is used to explain the reason for something (Behavioral Science #5)

—N—

national defense—(noun) the protection of a country from attack by another country (Economics #2)

natural resource—(noun) any product of nature; examples are water, coal and trees (Geography #1, #3)

Nazi Party—(noun) a racist political party which rose to power in Germany in 1933 under Adolf Hitler (History #6)

nutrition—(noun) food or nourishment (Geography #6)

—O—

official—(adjective) having to do with an important office or position (Geography #4, #5)

Orient—(noun) the Far East or eastern countries of Asia, including China and Japan, among others (Geography #5)

—P—

parallel—(noun) an imaginary line circling the earth in the same direction as the equator; a parallel marks latitude (Geography #2)

parliament—(noun) a group of elected and appointed people who make laws within a parliamentary system of government (Geography #3, #5)

peso—(noun) the Mexican unit of money (Geography #4)

physical feature—(noun) a form of the earth that can be seen; examples are a mountain, ocean or desert (Geography #1)

plantation—(noun) a big farm that often grows one crop and is worked by people living on it (History #2)

popular vote—(noun) the total vote of all the people in the country (Political Science #6)

population—(noun) the total number of people living in a particular country, city, or other area (Geography #4, #5, #6; History #2; Behavioral Science #5)

populous—(adjective) having many people; crowded (Geography #3)

poverty—(noun) being poor (Geography #4)

predict—(verb) to make a guess about what will happen (History #1; Behavioral Science #1)

prehistoric—(adjective) from the time before humans began writing down history (Economics #6)

Prime Meridian—(noun) the meridian of 0° longitude which runs through Greenwich, England (Geography #2)

prime minister—(noun) the head of a parliamentary government (Geography #3)

product—(noun) anything made, created or produced (Economics #3, #4, #5; Geography #1, #3, #5; History #4, #5)

production—(noun) making things (Economics #5; Geography #6)

productive—(adjective) making a large amount of something (Economics #1; Geography #5)

profit—(noun) money made after costs have been subtracted (Economics #5)

prosecutor—(noun) a lawyer in a trial who accuses someone of committing a crime (Political Science #5)

province—(noun) one of the ten regions of Canada (Geography #3)

psychology—(noun) the study of the human mind to find out how and why individuals act the way they do (Behavioral Science #1, #6)

pursuit—(noun) to follow or chase someone or something (Political Science #4)

—R—

racial—(adjective) having to do with a particular race of people (Behavioral Science #1)

racist—(adjective) having to do with the belief that one race of people is better than all others (History #5)

ratify—(verb) to formally approve or accept (Political Science #2)

raw material—(noun) an untreated product of nature used to manufacture a different product (Economics #4, History #5)

rebellion—(noun) the actions of a group of people who organize and arm themselves against their own government (Political Science #1)

recession—(noun) a condition of the economy when there is a slowing down of activity (Economics #3; History #5)

Reconstruction—(noun) the period in American history (1865-1876) when freedmen and others tried to rebuild the war-torn South after the Civil War (History #3)

relationship—(noun) a connection between two or more things (Behavioral Science #1)

repression—(noun) a defense mechanism that an individual uses to remove painful thoughts from his or her memory (Behavioral Science #6)

representative—(noun) a person chosen to do something for others (Political Science #6)

representative democracy—(noun) a government in which the citizens elect people to make decisions for them about public matters (Political Science #6)

research—(noun) careful study of a topic or a search for information (Behavioral Science #1)

reserve—(noun) something kept or stored for a special use in the future (Economics #6; Geography #4)

resource—(noun) a man-made or natural product (Geography #6)

retire—(verb) to stop working, usually because of old age (Behavioral Science #5)

revolution—(noun) the overthrow of a government by its citizens (History #5)

role—(noun) the rights, duties, and expected behavior of a person in a social group or society (Behavioral Science #1, #2, #4)

—S—

scapegoat—(noun) a person who is unfairly blamed for a problem that he or she did not cause (History #6)

seek—(verb) to try to get something or to look for something (History #2; Behavioral Science #1)

segregate—(verb) to keep apart from others; to separate by race (History #3)

segregation—(noun) the forced separation of races in schools, neighborhoods, jobs or public places (Political Science #3)

self-sufficient—(adjective) able to completely take care of oneself (Economics #4)

separation of powers—(noun) the division of duties and powers of the federal government into three branches: the executive, legislative, and judicial (Political Science #2)

services—(noun) useful work that someone is paid to do but which does not create products for sale (Economics #1, #3, #4, #6; History #4)

sharecropping—(noun) a system of farming in which a farmer grows crops on someone else's land and receives part of the crop as payment (History #3)

social—(adjective) anything having to do with people living in groups (Behavioral Science #1, #2, #4, #5)

social change—(noun) something new in how a society or its institutions work; some change in family, religious, or economic life, for example (Behavioral Science #4)

social role—(noun) the rights, duties, and expected behavior of a person in a social group or society (Behavioral Science #2, #4)

Social Security—(noun) a U.S. government program set up to provide monthly payments to old and needy people (Economics #2; Behavioral Science #5)

society—(noun) a very large group of people whose members share customs, beliefs, and institutions (Economics #5, #6; Geography #1, #4; Behavioral Science #1, #2, #3, #4)

sociology—(noun) the study of group behavior (Behavioral Science #1)

source—(noun) a point of original information; a source in the study of history could be any record or document that gives clues about an event or person (History #1)

spouse—(noun) marriage partner; husband or wife (Behavioral Science #5)

statutory law—(noun) the law passed by legislative bodies such as Congress or city councils (Political Science #4)

subject—(noun) an individual who is studied in an experiment (Behavioral Science #3)

Supreme Court—(noun) the highest court in the U.S. (Political Science #3)

survive—(verb) to keep living; to live through something difficult (History #2; Behavioral Science #2)

system—(noun) a plan made up of a set of connected facts, ideas, or other things (Behavioral Science #1)

—T—

take-home pay—(noun) the amount of money a worker receives after deductions have been taken out of his or her paycheck (Economics #2)

territory—(noun) land which is under the control of a far-away government; the land does not have the full rights of a state or province (History #4, #5, #6)

terrorist group—(noun) a group of people with a political goal who try to scare or terrorize other people (History #3)

testify—(verb) to state something based on knowledge or proof (Political Science #5)

topography—(noun) the physical features on the surface of land—lakes, mountains, roads and valleys, for example (Geography #1)

trait—(noun) a feature or quality that makes one person different from another (Behavioral Science #1)

—U—

unconscious—(noun) the unconscious part of the mind

(adjective) having to do with the part of the mind or a cause of behavior that we are not fully aware of (Behavioral Science #6)

unconstitutional—(adjective) not allowed by the Constitution (Political Science #3, #4)

undernourished—(adjective) underfed; having less food than is needed for growth and health (Geography #6)

unfold—(verb) to develop or come into view (History #2)

—V—

value—(noun) the worth, fair price or cost of something (Economics #1, #6)

values—(noun) beliefs or behaviors that are considered important to an individual, a group or a society (Geography #1; Behavioral Science #3)

veto—(verb) to turn something down or refuse to approve it (Political Science #2)

violate—(verb) to go against or fail to obey (Political Science #4)

—W—

withhold—(verb) to keep or hold back (Economics #2)

witness—(noun) a person who sees something happen and tells about it in court (Political Science #5)